The Best
Covered and
Kettle Grills
Cookbook Ever

Melanie Barnard

A John Boswell Associates/King Hill Pr...
HarperCollins*Publish...*

To Scott, the best outdoor cook ever.

Special thanks to the grill and smoker manufacturers who provided equipment for extensive recipe testing: Char-Broil, The Ducane Company, and the Hondo Smoker from New Braunfels Smoker Company. Gratitude also to the Barbecue Industry Association for their help and information, and to Susan Friedland and Susan Wyler for their continued support.

HarperCollins books may be purchased for educational, business, or sales promotional use. For information, please write: Special Markets Department, HarperCollins Publishers, Inc., 10 East 53rd Street, New York, NY 10022.

FIRST EDITION

Design: Barbara Cohen Aronica
Index: Maro Riofrancos

Library of Congress Cataloging-in-Publication Data

Barnard, Melanie.
    The best covered and kettle grills cookbook ever / Melanie
Barnard.—1st ed.
        p.   cm.
    "John Boswell Associates/King Hill Productions Book."
    Includes index.
    ISBN 0-06-017091-3
    1. Barbecue cookery.   I. Title.
TX840.B3837   1994
641.5'784—dc20   93-50759

94 95 96 97 98 HC 10 9 8 7 6 5 4 3 2 1

Contents

INTRODUCTION   1

Everything You Need to Know About Covered Grills   1

Types of Covered Grills   2

Smokers   3

Fuels   4

Aromatic Flavorings   4

Preparing the Charcoal Fire   6

Starter Methods   6

Controlling the Heat   8

The Right Temperature   8

Grill Safety   9

Tips for Great Grilling   10

Useful Attachments   11

Sources for Equipment and Supplies   12

CHAPTER ONE. APPETIZERS AND SNACKS   15

Great-tasting starters range from popular favorites—BBQ Wings and Wood-Fired White Clam Pizza—to more usual finger fare—Grilled Indonesian Chicken Satay and Grilled Broccoli and Potatoes with Beer Cheese Fondue.

CHAPTER TWO. CHICKEN, TURKEY, AND OTHER BIRDS 38

Variety rules the roost with recipes like Skewered Basque Chicken, Grilled Vietnamese Chicken Noodle Salad, Mahogany Turkey Legs, Grilled Turkey Taco Salad, and Grilled Game Hens with Mango Salsa.

CHAPTER THREE. BEEF, VEAL, AND VENISON 67

Plain steak and burgers will take a back seat to these tempting ways to treat your favorite meats: Teriyaki Flank Steak with Grilled Shiitake Mushrooms, Mother's Barbecued Meat Loaves, Grilled Tarragon-Mustard Veal Cutlets, Grilled Venison Steaks with Peppered Apples are just a sampling.

CHAPTER FOUR. PORK, HAM, SAUSAGE, AND RIBS 97

It's pig heaven! Whether fast cooked, slow cooked, smoked, or slathered with sauce, you'll want to try such finger-lickin' finds as Lemon and Fennel Grilled Pork Tenderloin, East St. Louis Barbecued Pork Steaks, and Molasses-Rum Country-Style Ribs.

CHAPTER FIVE. LAMB 120

Find out why lamb goes so well on the grill with great entertaining ideas like Hunan Barbecued Lamb, Lamb and Rosemary Spiedini, Grilled Moroccan Lamb and Couscous Salad, and Garlic and Oregano Boneless Leg of Lamb.

Contents

CHAPTER SIX. FISH AND SHELLFISH — 136

Recipes like Grilled Mahimahi with Toasted Coconut and Macadamia Butter, Grilled Mustard-Dill Salmon Roast, Blackened Red Snapper Fillets, and Grilled Shrimp Español show why seafood and smoke are a perfect match.

CHAPTER SEVEN. VEGETABLES — 168

Variety is the spice of life on the grill, too, with these healthful, garden-fresh delights. Pick from an assortment that includes Grilled Asparagus with Orange Vinaigrette, Corn in the Nude, Grilled Herbed Potato Salad, Grilled Ratatouille, and Grilled Acorn Squash with Cranberry Port Sauce.

CHAPTER EIGHT. SMOKING — 196

Slow and easy, home smokers offer great new flavor possibilities: Southern-Style Smoked Chicken, Hotter 'n Hell Smoked Beef Brisket, Smoked Apple-Sage Game Hens, and Home-Smoked Salmon, to name a few.

INDEX — 210

Introduction

Everything You Need to Know About Covered Grills

Though current haute cuisine would have us believe that grilling is practically a culinary art form, it is actually the easy way out when you want to cook fantastic tasting, relatively low-fat meals in a minimum of time with little fuss and practically no cleanup. And now, with the ready availability and sophistication of kettle grills—and other covered grills—and convenient gas grills, old-fashioned outdoor barbecuing is clearly just right for today's streamlined, upbeat life-styles.

Until a few years ago, covered grills were the oddity in a field of backyard cookers dominated by shallow, open grills with adjustable cooking grates. Covered grills have now become the most widely used method of grilling with charcoal, and gas models are available in a variety of price ranges. Smoking, probably the oldest form of covered cooking, is increasingly popular as home smokers have become better and more affordable in recent years.

There are several distinct advantages to the use of a covered grill.

Versatility—Covered grills combine range top and oven cooking. With the lid open, the grill gives off very high direct heat to the bottom of the food only. When the lid is closed,* the grill is both a direct heat stove top and an oven

*Note: All the recipes in this book are formulated for and were tested on *covered* grills.

in which the air circulates all around the food to permeate with even heat and flavorful smoke, while retaining moisture and juiciness.

Control—Unlike open grills, whose fire is at the mercy of wind and rain, air flow is controlled in covered grills, all but eliminating flare-ups and providing relatively steady heat that can be regulated and maintained for a longer period of time. In gas units, temperature is adjusted by controls outside of the grill, and charcoal fires are regulated by the amount of air allowed through the vents in the base and lid of the unit.

Efficiency—Because the heat does not immediately escape, but remains enclosed and reflects off the metal hood, covered grilling is a far more efficient use of fuel. In short cooking times, such as those for steaks or fish, covered grilling is only slightly faster than on conventional open grills, but with larger cuts such as roasts and whole birds, the cooking time is measurably less. In addition, when all vents are closed in a charcoal unit, the fire will quickly extinguish as the oxygen supply is eliminated. Gas units have on/off fuel efficiency and require approximately the same amount of preheating time as an indoor oven.

Types of Covered Grills

Covered grill styles are divided into kettle shape, rectangular, and square models. Most gas grills are rectangular, while charcoal grills are available in all shapes. Smokers, particularly offset firebox smokers, also double as conventional covered grills, too.

Charcoal grills give the most traditional "smoky" flavor to foods and allow for the greatest variety of aromatic flavor enhancers. They can be used anywhere, since charcoal fuel is easily portable. The major drawback is the messiness of preparing and lighting the fire, but some charcoal grills now have gas ignition systems to light the coals easily.

Gas grills offer "instant-on" with the push of a button, or at the most a light of a match from either an inground permanent gas line or a portable, refillable propane tank. Heat can be regulated like that of a gas range, usually in 2 or 3 settings. Rather than charcoal, gas grills are lined with ceramic briquettes, lava rocks, or other porous material heated by the gas jets to simulate charcoal. Each manufacturer designs the bricks or rocks in a different manner for optimum "grill" and "smoke," and many provide for the addition of damp wood chips or other aromatic flavor enhancers. Purists may still eschew gas grilling, but I find that a good gas grill is terrific for easy everyday cooking year round. At my house, the gas grill gets as much use as my oven and stove top.

Electric grills require only plugging in and turning on. Covered electric grills are now available, and the newer designs give good flavor with little effort and the most accurate temperature control of any type of grill, though they give the least "smoky" results.

Smokers

Smokers are available in two designs. The *water smoker,* a tall, cylindrical covered cooker with a fire pan for coals, a water pan, one or two grids, and a dome-shaped lid, is most common. The food is placed on the grid high above the coals, and the water pan is set in between to provide a cloud of continuous smoke to the food. The *offset smoker,* more like old-fashioned smoke-house smoking, is really two drum-shaped units in one, with the smaller one acting as the firebox and a conventional covered grill cooker. The large unit is attached slightly higher, and the smoke wafts upward around the food on the grids in it. Dampers control the heat and smoke in both types, and doors for fuel addition allow for the continuous long slow cooking that imparts the characteristic deep-smoked flavor. All types of smoking, as well as conventional grilling, can be done in an offset smoker.

Fuels

Charcoal briquettes—In the 1920s, auto magnate Henry Ford combined starch with charcoal scraps from his Model T plant and formed them into the now famous pillow-shaped briquettes, which he found to be a more efficient fuel for industrial use. Home cooks apparently agree, since charcoal briquettes—still made in much the same way from charcoal, anthracite, and sawdust—are the most widely used grilling fuel. Quality briquettes have the advantage of ready availability, moderate price, and good fire-starting capabilities. Avoid cheap briquettes that contain extra chemicals, since these can affect the taste of the food.

Hardwood lump charcoal—Like briquettes, lump charcoal is made by burning wood in a closed container until carbon is formed. Hardwood charcoal is left in the lump form of the original wood, and it contains no additives or fillers, thus creating a naturally hotter fire than briquettes. It is the preferred fuel of many barbecue aficionados, though it is more expensive and can be messy, since large pieces should be broken into chunks before use. However, unlike briquettes, which usually burn to ash after one use, hardwood charcoal can often be reused once or twice.

Hardwoods—The original grilling fuel, hardwoods are used less today as primary fuel because they are more difficult to ignite, burn quickly, and give off a more unpredictable heat. Oak, hickory, fruitwoods, and mesquite are the most common hardwoods, but their flavor can also be imparted when used as chips or chunks added to charcoal or briquettes.

Aromatic Flavorings

Wood chips, chunks, and dusts—Various sizes of hardwood are available to add to a charcoal or charcoal briquette fire, and even to some types of gas-fired grills. Chunks produce the strongest flavor and are good for foods cooked for a long time. Chips give off more smoke, but for a shorter period. Both should be thoroughly soaked in cold water for at least 30 minutes before adding to the fire just before cooking. Dusts, which are just finely ground chips, are tossed onto the hot coals or are used according to directions in gas grills when cooking time is very short. Any hardwood can be used as a flavor enhancer, but if you are gathering your own, avoid resinous woods, which give off an unpleasant aroma. The most common commercially available hardwood flavorings are:

- **Hickory:** The distinct, heavily smoky flavor reminiscent of bacon is well suited to assertive meats, such as pork and beef. Available in chips, chunks, and dusts.
- **Mesquite:** This scrub tree that grows wild in the Southwest produces a hot-burning, full-flavored charcoal, but the chips and chunks also impart the characteristic woodsy flavor to beef, lamb, vegetables, and fish steaks. Available in chips, chunks, and dusts.
- **Fruitwoods:** Cherry, apple, and peach are the most widely available, and the subtle aromas are especially good with fish, poultry, pork, and veal, as well as any recipe containing grilled fruit. Available in chips and chunks.

Other good wood chips for grilling, if you come across them, are alder, oak, walnut, or pecan.

Corncobs—You can buy dried corncobs, or dry your own in the sun for a few days or in a 200 degree oven for at least 12 hours. Be sure they are completely dried out, or they will rot during storage. Corncobs give off a flavor similar to hickory and are often used in long-cooked meats and smoked foods.

Grapevine twigs and cuttings—Long used in Italy and France, when soaked in water, then tossed onto the coals, these give off a subtle, winy, slightly sweet aroma particularly nice with fish and poultry.

Fresh herbs—Dampened fresh herb branches and sprigs, when added at the last minute to quickly grilled foods, such as steaks, chops, seafood, and vegetables, give a subtle flavor boost. Choose an herb that is also an ingredient in the recipe.

Seaweed—Washed and dried in the sun, seaweed is a natural flavor enhancer for all manner of seafood.

Preparing the Charcoal Fire

1. Lay in plenty of charcoal so that the bed is 2 or 3 inches deep and at least 2 inches larger in circumference than the food to be cooked. Depending upon the starter method used, the coals might first need to be heaped together in a loose pyramid for ignition, then spread out when ready to cook.

2. Unless otherwise directed by the manufacturer, leave the lid off the grill and the bottom vents open while preparing the fire.

3. Allow 30 to 40 minutes for the coals to reach cooking temperature.

4. If oiling the grill rack, do so before placing it over the fire.

5. Remember that if food is to be cooked longer than 1 hour, additional fuel will need to be added, allowing about 15 minutes for it to ignite.

Starter Methods (in order of my preference)

Gas ignition—An option from some grill manufacturers, this is as easy as a press of a button that sparks a gas ignition system in the bottom of the grill box to light the charcoal. Gas grills light in the same way, but the ignition sparks the gas jets, which in turn heat the lava rocks or bricks, taking 10 to 15 minutes to reach grilling temperature.

Electric fire starter—A metal loop element inserted in the center of a pyramid of coals heats red hot when plugged into an electrical outlet. After about 10 minutes, the coals nearest the loop will be ignited, and the element can be removed. The lit coals will then ignite the remaining coals in 10 or 15 minutes. Take care to let the element cool on a heatproof surface well away from traffic. Simple, inexpensive, and effective, these are limited by accessibility to an electric source.

Chimney starter—A perforated metal cylinder with a wood handle. Crumple newspaper into the bottom, then pile charcoal into the top. Remove the grill cooking rack and set the cylinder on the fuel grate or in the fire box. Ignite the newspaper, which will in turn ignite the charcoal in about 20 minutes. Use the handle to pour the hot coals carefully into the grill. These starters are especially suited to smaller fires. If you are building a large fire, you may need to add more coals to the lit ones in the grill. Wait another 20 minutes for them to reach the right temperature.

Kindling—Make a bed of rolled newspaper, then crisscross dry twigs over it and set a small pyramid of charcoal over the twigs. Ignite the newspaper. When the coals ignite, add more as needed for the size of the fire desired.

Fluid starters—Make a bed of one layer of coals, then soak with the fluid. Pile remaining coals on top in a pyramid. Light the bottom coals, which will light the others. Wait at least 30 minutes before cooking to allow the chemicals to burn off so they do not impart an off flavor to the food. *Never squirt liquid starter on a lit fire.*

Solid starters—These are wood or paraffin blocks impregnated with a combustible chemical. Presoaked charcoal briquettes also fall in this category. Place on the bottom of the pyramid and light. Though slower to start, these are easy to transport to a picnic.

Controlling the Heat

Charcoal fires usually take at least 30 minutes to reach hot cooking temperature. If a lower temperature is desired, cover the grill on a hot fire and partially close the vents, then wait for the coals to burn down. If the fire starts to go out, uncover, open the vents, and add more charcoal. Wait about 15 minutes until the proper heat has again been reached. When you are finished cooking, cover the grill and close the vents to cut off the air supply and thus extinguish the fire.

Most grilling is done over *direct heat* by placing the food on the cooking grate directly over the heat source. Foods that need to be cooked for a long time over medium or medium-low heat, such as large roasts and whole turkeys, are best done over *indirect heat,* in which the hot coals are pushed to the side or around the periphery of the fire box, or over reduced heat in a gas grill or by creating an indirect heat as your manufacturer suggests. The food is then placed on the grill away from the coals over a drip pan (heavy-duty foil shaped into a pan is fine) to catch grease drippings. Water or other liquid can be placed in this pan to encourage smoke and flavor. Smokers operate on the same principle, either by an indirect fire in an offset smoker or a water pan between the fire and the food in a water smoker.

Though food can be cooked without the lid in a covered grill, more control is achieved with the use of the cover. *All recipes in this book assume that the grill is covered during cooking.* Since even in a covered grill cooking times will vary according to the external weather conditions and the fire itself, a range is given for each recipe. Check after the minimum time.

The Right Temperature

- **Hot:** The coals glow red, and you can hold your hand 6 inches above the fire for no more than 3 seconds (425 to 475 degrees). Good for thin steaks and boneless poultry cutlets, or other small, quick-cooking foods.

- **Medium-hot:** The coals are gray, but with a red underglow, and you can hold your hand 6 inches above the coals for no more than 5 seconds (375 to 425 degrees). Good for poultry pieces and thick steaks or chops as well as sturdy vegetables.
- **Medium:** The coals are gray with only a hint of red, and you can hold your hand 6 inches above the fire for no more than 7 seconds (325 to 375 degrees). Good for small roasts, small whole birds, and delicate fruits and vegetables.
- **Low:** The coals are completely gray, and you can hold your hand 6 inches above the fire for 10 seconds (275 to 325 degrees). Because low coals threaten to go out completely, this type of heat is best accomplished on a charcoal grill by building a medium-hot indirect fire or by using a smoker. Gas grills can be regulated to low heat. Do the hand test over the area on which the food is to be placed. Good for large roasts and whole turkeys.

Grill Safety

- Position the grill in an open area well away from the house, dry leaves, or combustibles.
- Do not leave a grill unattended. Wind, dogs, and children can easily knock them over.
- Never add starter fluid after the fire is ignited.
- Keep a fire extinguisher, bucket of sand, or a source of water nearby in case of an emergency.
- Check coals for several hours after cooking in a grill and up to 48 hours in a smoker to be sure they are completely extinguished.
- Turn off the gas source and unplug from the electric source after each use of a gas or electric grill.
- When grilling, do not wear loose, flowing clothing that can catch fire.

- If using a meat, seafood, or poultry marinade as a table sauce, first boil for at least 3 minutes to destroy bacteria that may have been present in the raw state during marinating.

Tips for Great Grilling

- When a grill rack is oiled or sprayed with a nonstick coating, most foods can be cooked with no added fat.
- Keep the grill rack clean by brushing after each use with a stiff wire brush while the rack is still hot.
- Empty the ash catcher in a charcoal unit so that the bottom vents will remain unobstructed.
- To reduce sticking, heat the grill rack for a few minutes over the fire before cooking.
- Cut excess fat from all meats before grilling to reduce the chance of flare-ups when the grill is open.
- For optimum results and minimum cooking time, foods to be grilled should be at cool room temperature. Cold foods may burn on the outside before being cooked through.
- If using bamboo skewers, soak in cold water for at least 30 minutes to prevent burning.
- Turn foods with tongs or a wide spatula to avoid piercing them and losing juices.
- Make professional-looking cross-hatch grill marks by searing the food over a hot fire on a hot grill rack until brown lines appear, usually about 2 minutes. Rotate about 45 degrees and grill about 2 minutes longer. Turn over and repeat the process on the other side.
- Brush on thick or sweet sauces during the last 10 minutes or so of cooking time to prevent burning.

- Know the grill. Like a conventional oven, each has its own quirks and hot spots. Read the directions and follow for safety, best performance, and long grill life.
- Check foods after the minimum recommended cooking time, since grilling times are variable, even with a covered grill.

Useful Attachments

Grilling is a simple process and should remain so. There are only a few extras that are really worthwhile. These are:

- **Instant-reading thermometer,** for accurate temperature readings of meat and poultry.
- **Long-handled tongs, wide spatula, and basting brush,** for ease of turning.
- **Mitts that cover the wrist,** for safety.
- **Stiff wire brush,** for ease of cleaning the grill rack.

Sources for Equipment and Supplies

Equipment

THE BRINKMANN CORPORATION
4215 McEwen Road
Dallas, TX 75244
(214) 387-4939
Water smokers

CHAR-BROIL
Division of W.C. Bradley Company
P.O. Box 1240
Columbus, GA 31902-1240
(800) 352-4111
Gas grills

THE DUCANE COMPANY
800 Dutch Square Boulevard, Suite 200
Columbia, SC 29210
(803) 798-1600
Gas grills

MECO CORPORATION
1500 Industrial Road
Greenville, TN 37743-1171
(800) 251-7558
Charcoal and electric grills, water smokers

NEW BRAUNFELS SMOKER COMPANY (HONDO SMOKER)
P.O. Box 310096
New Braunfels, TX 78131
(800) 232-3398
Barbecue smokers and grills

WEBER-STEPHEN PRODUCTS CO.
200 E. Daniels Road
Palatine, IL 60067
(800) 446-1071
Charcoal kettles, gas grills, charcoal and gas accessories

Fuels and Accessories
CHARCOAL COMPANION
7955 Edgewater Drive
Oakland, CA 94621
(800) 521-0505
Wood chips, dry herbs, accessories

THE CONNECTICUT CHARCOAL COMPANY
P.O. Box 742
Westport, CT 06881
(203) 227-2101
Lump charcoal

COWBOY CHARCOAL COMPANY
P.O. Box 3770
Brentwood, TN 37024-3770
Lump charcoal

GRIFFO PRODUCTS, INC.
1400 North 30th
Quincy, IL 62301
(800) 426-1286
Wood chips and accessories

HICKORY SPECIALTIES, INC.
P.O. Box 1669
Brentwood, TN 37027
(615) 373-2581
Charcoal briquettes, wood smoking chips, ceramic gas grill briquettes

THE KINGSFORD PRODUCTS COMPANY
1221 Broadway-17th Floor
Oakland, CA 94612
(510) 271-7000
Charcoal briquettes, lighter fluid, charcoal grills

T. S. RAGSDALE COMPANY, INC.
P.O. Box 937
Lake City, SC 29560
(803) 394-8567
Charcoal briquettes

Chapter One
Appetizers and Snacks

Most of the tasty tidbits in this chapter cook in such short order that they make a perfect prelude to any grilled main course. Also, they are designed to be flexible in the type of heat of fire to be used, so that the fire that you prepare for the main event will do nicely for the first course, too.

Cocktail food, since it is served in tiny portions, is at its best when it is packed with a lot of flavor and presented with flair. Grilling emphasizes both. From delicate individual Grilled Melon and Prosciutto kebabs to hearty BBQ Wings, and from exotic little Grilled Stuffed Grape Leaves to Quick Grilled Pepperoni and Cheese Pizza for the kid in everyone, make the most of your grill with an appetizer or snack.

Grilled appetizers should be freshly cooked, but all of the work in preparation can be done well in advance. That leaves only the wonderful smells that will entice your guests to gather about the grill. Another great idea is a grilling cocktail party, in which the barbecue grill becomes the focus of conversation as well as the vehicle for producing terrific, tasty, and very simple food. Set up a table not far from the grill, stock it with lots of napkins and small plates, then cook up your party.

Yogurt- and Mint-Grilled Chicken Kebabs

These kebabs make a terrific hot appetizer. They can also be served as a main course over curried rice. To do so, simply cut the chicken into 1½-inch chunks and grill about 12 to 14 minutes. I like boneless chicken breast for its light flavor, but boneless thighs can be used, too. Bamboo skewers about 4 to 6 inches in length make a pretty presentation, but small metal skewers will work as well.

8 Servings

---

1 cup plain yogurt
2 teaspoons ground coriander
1 teaspoon ground cumin
½ cup chopped fresh mint, plus sprigs
　for garnish

½ cup chopped red onion
½ teaspoon salt
¼ teaspoon cayenne, or more to taste
1 pound skinless, boneless chicken
　breasts, cut into 1-inch chunks

---

1. In a shallow dish just large enough to hold the chicken, combine the yogurt, coriander, cumin, chopped mint, onion, salt, and cayenne. Add the chicken and turn to coat all sides. Cover and refrigerate at least 1 hour and up to 4 hours.

2. Prepare a hot fire in a covered charcoal or gas grill. If using bamboo skewers, soak them in cold water for at least 30 minutes. Thread about 2 pieces of chicken onto each skewer. Grill, turning occasionally, until the chicken is browned outside and white to the center, about 10 to 12 minutes.

3. Serve the chicken kebabs hot or warm on a platter garnished with mint sprigs.

Grilled Indonesian Chicken Satay

This is a simplified version of what is often a complex list of ingredients, but the end result is just as terrific and always one of the first nibbles to go at a cocktail party. If you want to serve these as a main course, cut the chicken into slightly bigger pieces and assume the recipe will serve about four people with rice and a salad.

8 Servings

---

1 pound skinless, boneless chicken thighs or breasts

¼ cup plus 2 tablespoons creamy peanut butter

¼ cup lime juice

3 tablespoons soy sauce

1 tablespoon minced fresh ginger

2 garlic cloves, minced

½ teaspoon crushed hot red pepper

---

1. Cut the chicken into 1-inch pieces. In a medium bowl, whisk together all of the remaining ingredients. Add the chicken and stir to coat completely. Cover and refrigerate at least 1 hour and up to 6 hours.

2. Prepare a hot fire in a covered charcoal or gas grill. Oil the grill rack. Remove the chicken from the marinade but do not pat dry. Thread on small metal skewers or bamboo skewers that have been soaked in water for at least 30 minutes, 2 pieces to each individual skewer. Grill, turning occasionally, until the chicken is white throughout with a browned exterior, about 8 to 10 minutes.

Grilled Sesame Chicken Tidbits with Sweet and Sour Dipping Sauce

Cutting the chicken into strips, then threading it onto small bamboo skewers, makes a pretty and easy-to-serve party tidbit. The dipping sauce takes just a few minutes to throw together.

6 Servings

---

2 tablespoons vegetable oil
½ cup lemon juice
½ teaspoon salt
¼ teaspoon freshly ground pepper
1 pound thinly sliced chicken or
　turkey breast cutlets

¾ cup apricot preserves
2 teaspoons grated lemon zest
1 teaspoon Dijon mustard
¼ cup sesame seeds

---

1. In a shallow dish just large enough to hold the chicken, combine the oil, ¼ cup of the lemon juice, the salt, and the pepper. Add the chicken and turn to coat both sides. Let stand 30 minutes or refrigerate up to 2 hours.

2. In a small saucepan, heat the preserves, lemon zest, mustard, and remaining ¼ cup lemon juice over medium-low heat, stirring, until the preserves are melted, about 4 minutes. Let cool to room temperature. (The dipping sauce can be made a day ahead and refrigerated, but return it to room temperature to serve.)

3. Prepare a hot fire in a covered charcoal or gas grill. Soak 18 bamboo skewers in cold water for at least 30 minutes. Remove the chicken from the marinade and sprinkle both sides of the cutlets with the sesame seeds, pressing them lightly with your hands to help them adhere. Using a large, sharp knife, cut the chicken into ½-inch strips. Thread 1 or 2 strips of chicken onto each skewer, weaving to secure the meat.

4. Grill, turning once, until the chicken is just cooked through and the sesame seeds are golden brown, about 4 minutes total. Serve the chicken tidbits on their skewers, accompanied by the dipping sauce.

BBQ Wings

This barbecued variation on the now-classic "Buffalo" theme is such a popular appetizer, I find everyone eats so many that it might as well be the main course! The traditional blue cheese dip and celery sticks are the ideal refreshing foil for the fiery hot wings.

6 to 8 Servings

---

2 tablespoons lemon juice
1 tablespoon vegetable oil
1 tablespoon Worcestershire sauce
2 teaspoons hot pepper sauce
18 chicken wings (about 2½ pounds)

3 cups shredded iceberg lettuce
1 cup bottled creamy blue cheese dip
   or salad dressing
12 to 16 celery sticks

---

1. In a small dish, combine the lemon juice, oil, Worcestershire, and hot pepper sauce. Place the chicken wings in a shallow dish and pour the sauce over them. Toss the wings to coat completely with sauce. Let stand 30 minutes.

2. Prepare a hot fire in a covered charcoal or gas grill. Cook the wings, turning often and brushing with any remaining sauce, until the skin is browned and crisp and the chicken is no longer pink near the bone, about 14 to 18 minutes.

3. On a large platter, make a bed of the lettuce and place the chicken wings on top. Serve the blue cheese dip in a separate ramekin and arrange the celery sticks to the side of the chicken.

Grilled Tuna Kebabs with Wasabi
and Pickled Ginger

Wasabi powder, a Japanese horseradish condiment, and pickled ginger, also known as gari, *are available at Asian markets and in the specialty foods section of many large supermarkets. Reconstitute the wasabi powder according to package directions, usually just enough water to make a paste. Both of these condiments are very spicy, but just right for the tuna. If you want to serve this as a main course, grill the tuna steaks without cutting them into chunks, and assume it will feed four.*

6 to 8 Servings

½ cup soy sauce

2 tablespoons mirin (rice wine) or dry sherry

2 tablespoons vegetable oil

1 tablespoon Asian sesame oil

1 pound fresh tuna steaks, cut 1 inch thick

2 bunches of scallions

½ cup pickled ginger slices

½ cup reconstituted wasabi

---

1. In a shallow dish just large enough to hold the tuna, combine 2 tablespoons of the soy sauce with the mirin, vegetable oil, and sesame oil. Cut the tuna into 1-inch pieces. Trim the scallions, leaving 2 inches of green. Add the tuna and scallions to the marinade and stir to coat all sides. Let stand 30 minutes.

2. Prepare a medium-hot fire in a covered charcoal or gas grill. Soak 12 to 16 small bamboo skewers in cold water for at least 30 minutes.

3. Thread a piece of tuna and scallion onto each skewer; reserve marinade in dish. Grill, turning often and brushing with remaining marinade, until the tuna is just cooked through and the scallions are softened and lightly browned, about 7 to 9 minutes.

4. Serve the tuna skewers on a platter with small dishes of the pickled ginger, wasabi, and remaining 6 tablespoons soy sauce for dipping.

Grilled Scallop and Grapefruit Kebabs

Skewer these tidbits on individual small bamboo skewers for a pretty presentation. Use sea scallops of uniform size for easiest cooking. Section the grapefruit over a bowl and you will probably have enough juice to use in the recipe.

6 to 8 Servings

---

3 tablespoons grapefruit juice
2 tablespoons vegetable oil
2 tablespoons tequila
1 teaspoon ground cumin
¼ teaspoon cayenne

¼ teaspoon salt
1 pound sea scallops
2 small grapefruits, peeled and
   sectioned

---

1. In a shallow dish just large enough to hold the scallops and grapefruit, combine the grapefruit juice, oil, tequila, cumin, cayenne, and salt. Add the scallops and grapefruit and turn to coat. Let stand 30 minutes.

2. Prepare a medium fire in a covered charcoal or gas grill. Soak 16 to 20 small bamboo skewers in cold water for at least 30 minutes. Thread a scallop and a grapefruit section onto each skewer; reserve any marinade left in dish.

3. Grill, turning occasionally and brushing with remaining marinade, until the grapefruit are tinged with brown and the scallops are cooked through, about 8 to 10 minutes total.

Grilled Shrimp Cocktail

This is as easy as it is tasty. Serve the shrimp hot from the grill and give your guests a choice of the zippy dipping salsa or lemon wedges. Ask the fishmonger to shell and devein the shrimp, leaving the tails intact to use as a "dipper."

6 to 8 Servings

1 cup bottled chili sauce

2 tablespoons prepared white horseradish

¼ cup plus 1 tablespoon lemon juice

¼ cup olive oil

1 teaspoon Tabasco or other hot sauce

1½ pounds shelled and deveined large shrimp, with tails intact

2 to 3 lemons

1. In a small bowl, stir together the chili sauce, horseradish, and 1 tablespoon of the lemon juice. Let the dipping sauce stand 30 minutes, or cover and refrigerate up to 24 hours.

2. In a shallow dish just large enough to hold the shrimp, combine the remaining ¼ cup lemon juice with the olive oil and Tabasco and mix well. Add the shrimp and turn to coat completely. Let stand 30 minutes.

3. Prepare a hot fire in a covered charcoal or gas grill. Thread the shrimp through the middle onto single or double skewers. Grill, turning once, until the shrimp are pink and firm to the touch, 4 to 6 minutes total.

4. Cut the lemons into wedges. Serve the shrimp on a platter surrounded by lemon wedges, with a bowl of the dipping sauce in the center.

Sweet and Sour Cocktail Franks

You can use little cocktail frankfurters as suggested here, or cut good-quality beef or turkey hot dogs into 1-inch chunks. I find it easiest to cook these on large metal skewers, then remove the franks to a platter and serve with toothpicks for picking up and dipping the grilled franks and peppers.

8 Servings

---

1 cup peach preserves
¼ cup white wine vinegar
1 tablespoon grated fresh ginger
1 red bell pepper

1 green bell pepper
2 tablespoons vegetable oil
½ pound cocktail frankfurters

---

1. In a small saucepan, heat the preserves, vinegar, and ginger over medium-low heat, stirring, until the preserves are melted, about 4 minutes. (The sauce can be made a day ahead and refrigerated. Reheat until warm to serve.) Cut the bell peppers into 1½-inch chunks and brush with the vegetable oil.

2. Prepare a hot fire in a covered charcoal or gas grill. Thread the pepper chunks and the frankfurters onto metal skewers. Grill, turning occasionally, until the peppers are softened and the franks and peppers are lightly browned, about 7 to 9 minutes total.

3. Remove the franks and peppers from the skewers and place in a shallow dish with a bowl of the warm sauce in the center for dipping.

Grilled Rumaki

This is an old favorite made new on the grill. Use small bamboo skewers, then heap them onto a platter for serving. If your skewers are the long ones, cut each in half.

8 Servings

¼ cup dry sherry
¼ cup soy sauce
2 garlic cloves, crushed in a press
1 tablespoon vegetable oil
1 teaspoon honey
1 teaspoon grated fresh ginger

1 pound chicken livers, rinsed and dried
1 (5½-ounce) can water chestnuts, cut in half
12 to 15 slices bacon, halved (about ⅔ pound)

---

1. In a shallow dish just large enough to hold the livers and water chestnuts, combine the sherry, soy sauce, garlic, oil, honey, and ginger. Cut any large livers in half. There should be 24 to 30 pieces. Place the livers and water chestnuts in the dish, stirring to coat all over. Let stand 30 minutes or refrigerate up to 2 hours.
2. Prepare a medium-hot fire in a covered charcoal or gas grill. Soak 24 to 30 bamboo skewers in cold water for at least 30 minutes. Wrap a bacon piece around a liver and a water chestnut half, then secure on a skewer. Repeat to use all ingredients.
3. Grill, turning often, until the bacon is crisp and the livers are cooked through, about 9 to 12 minutes.

Grilled Garlic Crostini

This is far too good merely to be called garlic toast, but it is far too easy to be saved for special events. The grill-roasted garlic from step 1 is also wonderful as a spread on baked potatoes and other vegetables.

6 Servings

---

6 large garlic cloves, unpeeled
¼ cup plus 1 tablespoon extra-virgin
   olive oil

1 loaf of Italian bread (about 12
   ounces), cut diagonally into ½-inch
   slices

---

1. Prepare a medium-hot fire in a covered charcoal or gas grill. Brush the garlic cloves lightly with some of the olive oil, then wrap them in heavy-duty aluminum foil to make a small packet. Set the garlic packet at the edge of the grill and cook, turning occasionally, until the garlic is very soft, about 15 to 20 minutes.
2. Squeeze the softened garlic from the peel into a small bowl. Stir in the remaining olive oil, mashing the garlic to a paste.
3. Grill the bread, turning to lightly toast both sides, about 1 to 1½ minutes total. Brush both sides of the grilled bread lightly with the garlic oil.

Grilled Herbed Polenta

Polenta, the Italian version of lowly cornmeal mush, is haute cuisine these days, and for good reason. It tastes terrific, especially when grilled.

8 to 10 Servings

---

2 cups chicken broth
1 cup polenta or yellow cornmeal
1 cup cold water
1 tablespoon chopped fresh sage or 1 teaspoon dried
3 tablespoons unsalted butter
¼ cup grated Parmesan cheese

½ teaspoon freshly ground pepper
Salt
3 tablespoons olive oil
3 cups marinara sauce

3 to 4 fresh sage branches, optional

---

1. In a 2-quart saucepan set over medium heat, bring the broth to a boil. Whisk the polenta into the cold water until smooth and free of lumps, then slowly whisk into the boiling broth. Reduce the heat to low and cook, stirring almost constantly, until the mixture is very thick and pulls away from the sides of the pan, 12 to 15 minutes. Stir in the sage, butter, cheese, and pepper. Season with salt to taste. Scrape the polenta into a buttered 10-inch pie plate. Let cool, then refrigerate at least 30 minutes or up to 4 hours, until firm.

2. Prepare a medium-hot fire in a covered charcoal or gas grill. Oil the grill rack. Cut the polenta into 8 or 10 wedges and brush on all sides with the olive oil. In a saucepan, bring the marinara sauce to a simmer.

3. If using the sage branches, dampen them under cold water and toss them onto the coals just before cooking. Grill the polenta, turning once carefully with a spatula, until browned and crisp, about 6 to 8 minutes total. Serve the polenta with the marinara sauce spooned on top.

Grilled Stuffed Grape Leaves

These little tidbits are so simple and quick to grill, but make a big splash at a summer cocktail party. Look for grape leaves in a jar in the specialty foods section of the market.

6 to 8 Servings

---

30 grape leaves

¼ cup olive oil

1 tablespoon chopped fresh oregano or
  1 teaspoon dried

1 pound feta cheese, crumbled

3 or 4 handfuls grapevine cuttings,
  optional

---

1. Rinse the grape leaves and pat them dry. In a small dish, combine the olive oil and oregano. Lay the grape leaves flat on a work surface and brush the surface with some of the oregano oil. Place about 1 tablespoon of cheese in the center of each grape leaf and fold up to enclose the cheese completely. Brush the outside of the packet with additional oregano oil. (The packets can be prepared to this point several hours ahead and refrigerated. Return to room temperature before cooking.)

2. Prepare a medium-hot fire in a covered charcoal or gas grill. Oil the grill rack. If using the grapevine cuttings, soak in cold water for at least 30 minutes. Just before cooking, toss the cuttings onto the coals.

3. Grill the grape leaf packets, turning once carefully with tongs or a spatula, until the grape leaves are lightly tinged with brown and the cheese is softened, about 2 minutes total.

Grilled Cheese en Carozza

A thoroughly Italian classic, this is a cross between a grilled cheese sandwich and French toast. Here, instead of frying, the egg-battered cheese sandwich is grilled, then cut into quarters to serve as an appetizer with a marinara sauce.

8 Servings

---

4 eggs
3 tablespoons milk
½ teaspoon dried oregano
¼ teaspoon salt
¼ teaspoon freshly ground pepper

8 slices of firm white sandwich bread
6 ounces thinly sliced Fontina or mozzarella cheese
2 ounces very thinly sliced prosciutto
2 cups marinara sauce

---

1. Prepare a medium-hot fire in a covered charcoal or gas grill. Oil the grill rack.

2. In a shallow dish, beat the eggs with the milk, oregano, salt, and pepper. Make 4 sandwiches with the bread, cheese, and prosciutto. Dip the sandwiches into the egg, turning carefully if necessary to allow both sides of the bread to absorb the egg. Heat the marinara sauce to a simmer on the stove or in a pan set at the edge of the grill.

3. Grill the sandwiches, turning once carefully with a wide spatula, until golden brown and with grill marks, about 7 to 9 minutes total.

4. To serve, cut into quarters and arrange on a platter around a bowl of the warm marinara sauce for dipping.

Quick Grilled Pepperoni and Cheese Pizza

This is about as easy as it gets, but grilling these pizzas lifts convenience food to a new status. Cut in small wedges, it is an appetizer, but your family will clamor for these pizzas for supper, too. All sorts of other toppings will work as well, such as leftover cooked vegetables or other types of cheese.

4 Servings

---

1 cup prepared pizza or spaghetti sauce

4 ounces thinly sliced pepperoni (about 1 cup)

6 ounces shredded mozzarella cheese (about 1½ cups)

4 individual pizza bread shells (two 8-ounce packages)

---

1. Prepare a medium-hot fire in a covered charcoal or gas grill. Oil the grill rack. Divide the sauce, pepperoni, and cheese among the pizza bread shells.

2. Grill the pizzas without turning until the cheese melts and the bottom is browned, about 7 to 10 minutes.

3. Use a pizza cutter to cut each pizza into 6 wedges. Serve while hot.

Wood-Fired White Clam Pizza

Wood-fired pizza ovens are all the rage in trendy trattorias these days. That same appealing, lightly charred flavor can be obtained at home so easily with refrigerated pizza dough and your backyard covered grill. Be sure to make plenty, because these will go fast.

6 to 8 Servings

---

3 tablespoons olive oil
3 garlic cloves, minced
¼ teaspoon crushed hot red pepper
1 (10-ounce) tube refrigerated pizza
  dough
⅔ cup chopped fresh clams or 1 (10-ounce) can chopped or baby clams, drained

1 tablespoon chopped fresh oregano or
  1 teaspoon dried
2 tablespoons grated Parmesan cheese

2 to 3 handfuls mesquite wood chips
  or grapevine cuttings, optional

---

1. Prepare a medium-hot fire in a covered charcoal or gas grill. Oil the grill rack. If using the mesquite chips or grapevine cuttings, soak them in cold water for at least 30 minutes.

2. In a small bowl, mix 2 tablespoons of the olive oil with the garlic and hot pepper. Let the garlic oil stand 15 minutes. Meanwhile, unroll the pizza dough and place on a baking sheet. Use the palm of your hand or a rolling pin to pat the dough into a rough 14-inch square. Brush the dough with about ½ tablespoon olive oil, then use a sharp knife to cut the dough into 4 even pieces.

3. If using the wood chips or vines, toss them onto the coals just before grilling or add to the gas grill according to the manufacturer's directions. Grill the pizza dough, oiled side down, for 3 to 4 minutes. Brush the top of the dough with the

---

remaining olive oil and turn the dough with a wide spatula. Working quickly, brush the garlic oil over the grilled sides of the pizza dough. Sprinkle the clams, oregano, and cheese evenly over the dough. Grill until the bottoms of the pizzas are crisp and the topping is bubbly and tinged with brown, about 3 minutes longer.

4. To serve as finger food, use a sharp knife to cut the pizzas into 1½-inch squares. Serve warm. (If necessary, the pizzas can be rewarmed and recrisped over low coals or in a 400 degree oven for a few minutes.)

Grilled Quesadillas

You can make these as hot or mild as you like depending upon the type of cheese and style of salsa that you select. However you do it, make plenty, since they are addictive.

8 Servings

---

8 ounces Monterey Jack cheese, with or without jalapeño peppers
¼ cup chopped cilantro

8 flour tortillas (7- or 8-inch size)
1½ cups bottled salsa, hot or mild

---

1. Prepare a medium fire in a covered charcoal or gas grill. Oil the grill rack. Sprinkle the cheese and the cilantro on 4 of the tortillas, leaving a ½-inch border all around. Top with the remaining tortillas to make "sandwiches." Press the edges together with dampened fingers.

2. Grill the quesadillas, turning once carefully with a spatula, until the tortillas are lightly browned and the cheese is melted, about 4 to 6 minutes total.

3. Cut each of the quesadillas into 6 or 8 wedges and serve with the salsa for dipping.

Grilled Cheese and Bean Tostadas

You can vary the filling according to what you like and what you have on hand. Cut the tostadas into quarters for appetizer portions, or serve as an open-faced sandwich for an informal main course.

10 Servings

---

8 corn tortillas
1½ cups canned refried beans
3 ounces (¾ cup) shredded Cheddar cheese
3 ounces (¾ cup) shredded Monterey Jack cheese

1 avocado, peeled and sliced
1½ cups shredded iceberg lettuce
1½ cups bottled salsa or taco sauce

---

1. Prepare a medium-hot fire in a covered charcoal or gas grill. Oil the grill rack. Grill one side of the tortillas until just crisp, about 1 minute. Remove from the grill to a baking sheet, grilled side up.

2. Partially mash the beans to break them up. Spread about 3 tablespoons of the beans over each tortilla. Sprinkle the Cheddar and Monterey Jack cheeses over the beans and top with avocado slices. Set the tostadas on the grill and cook until the cheese melts and the avocados are softened, about 3 minutes.

3. Cut the tostadas into quarters, then top with the lettuce and a drizzle of salsa. Pass the remaining salsa separately.

Grilled Tomato and Basil Bruschetta

This simple recipe is dependent upon quality ingredients: extra-virgin olive oil, ripe tomatoes, fresh basil, and good bread. Since the cooking time is very short, any temperature fire will do, so be sure to include it as a starter for many of your summer cookouts.

8 Servings

¼ cup extra-virgin olive oil

2 large garlic cloves, minced

1 pound ripe tomatoes—peeled, seeded, and chopped

⅓ cup chopped sweet white or red onion

⅓ cup coarsely chopped fresh basil, plus leaves for garnish

2 tablespoons balsamic vinegar

½ teaspoon salt

½ teaspoon coarsely ground black pepper

8 slices of crusty Italian bread, cut ½ inch thick

1 cup shredded mozzarella cheese

1. In a small bowl, combine the olive oil and garlic. Let the garlic oil stand 15 minutes. In a medium bowl, combine the tomatoes, onion, chopped basil, vinegar, salt, pepper, and 2 tablespoons of the garlic oil. Stir gently to mix. Let stand 15 to 30 minutes to allow the flavors to blend.

2. Prepare a medium or hot fire in a covered charcoal or gas grill. Brush both sides of the bread with the remaining 2 tablespoons garlic oil. Grill until lightly toasted on one side, about 45 seconds. Turn the bread over and quickly spoon the tomato mixture over the toasted side. Sprinkle the cheese on top.

3. Grill until the bread is toasted, the cheese is melted, and the tomato mixture is slightly warmed, about 45 seconds.

Grilled Melon and Prosciutto

You can buy a whole melon and cut it up yourself, but it is easier to buy a mix of cantaloupe and honeydew pieces from the salad bar of the market. If you can't find walnut or hazelnut oil, substitute all vegetable oil. Good domestic prosciutto is now available at far less cost than the imported type, and it works very nicely in this light summer hors d'oeuvre.

8 Servings

---

2 tablespoons walnut or hazelnut oil
1 tablespoon vegetable oil
2 tablespoons lime juice
1 tablespoon honey
¼ teaspoon salt

¼ teaspoon freshly ground pepper
4 cups melon chunks, about 1 inch
  each (no watermelon)
6 ounces very thinly sliced prosciutto
Lime wedges, for garnish

---

1. Prepare a medium fire in a covered charcoal or gas grill. Oil the grill rack. Soak 24 small bamboo skewers in cold water for at least 30 minutes.

2. In a shallow dish just large enough to hold the melon, combine the walnut oil, vegetable oil, lime juice, honey, salt, and pepper. Add the melon and turn to coat completely.

3. Wrap each melon piece in a small strip or piece of prosciutto, then thread 2 or 3 wrapped melon pieces onto each wet bamboo skewer. Reserve any marinade left in the dish.

4. Grill, turning once or twice and brushing with any remaining marinade, until the melon is beginning to soften and is lightly tinged with brown, about 5 minutes. Serve garnished with the lime wedges.

Appetizers and Snacks

Grilled French Toast with Maple-Mustard Sauce

This grilled version of French toast makes a fine appetizer, but it is also wonderful for a Sunday breakfast or brunch with maple syrup and grilled bacon or sausage patties.

8 Servings

---

3 tablespoons butter
3 tablespoons maple syrup
1 tablespoon Dijon mustard
4 eggs
3 tablespoons milk

¼ teaspoon salt
¼ teaspoon freshly ground pepper
8 slices of French bread, cut on the diagonal about ½ inch thick

---

1. In a small saucepan, melt the butter with the syrup and mustard over medium-low heat, stirring, until smooth and hot, about 3 minutes. Keep warm. (The sauce can be made a day ahead and reheated to serve.)

2. Prepare a medium-hot fire in a covered charcoal or gas grill. Oil the grill rack. In a shallow dish, beat the eggs with the milk, salt, and pepper. Dip the bread into the egg, turning to allow both sides to absorb the egg.

3. Grill the French toast, turning once, until golden brown and puffed, about 7 to 9 minutes total.

4. To serve, cut the grilled breads in half or in thirds or quarters and serve on a platter around a small bowl of the warm sauce.

Grilled Broccoli and Potatoes with Beer Cheese Fondue

This is a great appetizer for a chilly early autumn evening, but it can also serve as an informal meatless main course. Because the cheese fondue is stabilized by a roux, or flour and butter base, it can be kept warm at the side of the grill without danger of separating.

6 to 8 Servings

1 pound small red potatoes	1¼ cups milk
1 large bunch of broccoli	1½ cups beer (12 ounces)
4 tablespoons unsalted butter	1 pound Cheddar cheese, shredded
¼ cup all-purpose flour	1 teaspoon Worcestershire sauce
1½ teaspoons dry mustard	½ teaspoon Tabasco, or more to taste

1. If the potatoes are larger than 1½ inches in diameter, cut them in half. Trim the broccoli into florets with 2-inch stems. In a large pot of lightly salted water, cook the potatoes for 5 minutes. Add the broccoli and cook 2 minutes. Drain the vegetables and rinse well under cold water. (The vegetables can be parboiled early in the day.)

2. In a medium saucepan, melt the butter. Add the flour and cook over medium heat, stirring constantly, for 1 minute. Stir in the mustard and cook 1 minute. Gradually whisk in the milk and beer. Bring to a boil, stirring constantly. Reduce the heat to medium-low and simmer, stirring, for 2 minutes.

3. Reduce the heat to low and add the cheese, 1 cup at a time, whisking or stirring until melted. Season with the Worcestershire and Tabasco. (The fondue can be made early in the day. Cover and refrigerate, but return to room temperature before continuing.)

4. Prepare a medium-hot barbecue fire in a covered charcoal or gas grill. Skewer the potatoes and broccoli alternately on metal skewers. Grill, turning often, until the vegetables are nicely browned and tender, about 5 minutes. Meanwhile, reheat the cheese fondue gently in a fondue pot or attractive flameproof casserole, set over the lowest possible heat or at the side of the barbecue fire.

5. Slip the vegetables off their skewers and arrange on a platter. Provide long forks for dipping into the warm fondue.

Chapter Two

Chicken, Turkey, and Other Birds

We Americans eat more chicken as a main course than anything else, and the grill is the perfect way to liven up the naturally mild flavor of this versatile bird and its feathered relatives. Whether you choose traditional All-American Barbecued Chicken or contemporary Grilled Turkey Taco Salad, covered kettle and gas grilling is the ideal way to cook all forms of poultry.

Except for thin breast fillets that cook very quickly over high heat, use medium-high or medium coals and be sure to test for doneness. Oiling the grill rack allows skinless pieces to cook without sticking. Covered grills allow even large whole birds to cook to a juicy doneness, so precooking indoors is no longer necessary.

All poultry should be cooked until the meat is white throughout and the juices run clear. Avoid overcooking, though, which will dry it out. Large pieces can be tested with a thermometer; they should register 170 degrees for white meat and 180 degrees for dark meat.

If the bird is basted as it grills, be sure to stop a minute or two before the meat is done, so the sauce clinging to it has time to cook. And if you plan to use a basting sauce or marinade as a table sauce, boil it first for at least 3 minutes to cook through.

All-American Barbecued Chicken

This is the finger-lickin' barbecued chicken that has made the American backyard barbecue famous. Choose any bone-in chicken parts that you like, but have the butcher cut any large breast pieces in half crosswise for more even cooking and easy serving.

8 Servings

---

6 pounds cut-up chicken
3 cups All-American Barbecue Sauce
(page 42)

---

1. Prepare a medium fire in a covered charcoal or gas grill. Grill the chicken, skin side down, for 10 minutes. Turn skin side up and grill 5 minutes.
2. Brush with some of the sauce and grill, brushing with additional sauce, until the chicken is no longer pink and the juices run clear when pricked with a knife tip, about 20 to 30 minutes longer. (White meat parts will take less time than the legs and thighs.)

Grilled Whole Chicken Stuffed with Lemons and Sage

Pushing the coals to the side to create an indirect heat source here ensures that the chicken will be cooked through with a moist and juicy interior and crispy, golden-brown skin. Adding white wine and fresh sage leaves to the drip pan creates a flavorful smokiness.

4 Servings

---

1 broiler-fryer chicken, about 3 pounds	¼ cup chopped fresh sage or 4 teaspoons dried
⅔ cup dry white wine	⅓ cup water
2 tablespoons olive oil	1 lemon, cut into 8 wedges
2 tablespoons lemon juice	Lemon slices
½ teaspoon salt	Sprigs of fresh sage, optional
¼ teaspoon freshly ground pepper	

---

1. Remove the giblets from the chicken and discard or reserve for other uses. In a bowl just large enough to hold the chicken, combine ⅓ cup of the wine with the olive oil, lemon juice, salt, pepper, and half of the chopped sage. Add the chicken and turn to coat completely. Cover and refrigerate, turning occasionally, for at least 3 hours and up to 24 hours.

2. Prepare a medium fire in a covered charcoal or gas grill. If using a charcoal grill, carefully lift up the grate with a fireproof mitt and push the coals to one side with a long-handled spoon or spatula. Oil the grill rack. Place an aluminum foil drip pan to the side opposite the coals and pour the remaining ⅓ cup wine, ⅓ cup water, and half of the remaining sage into the drip pan. Remove the chicken from the marinade, but reserve the marinade. Stuff the cavity of the chicken with the remaining chopped sage and the lemon wedges. For a neater look, tie the legs together.

3. Set the chicken, breast side down, on the grill over the drip pan. Grill 20 minutes, then brush with some of the marinade and turn breast side up. If using a gas grill, reduce the heat to medium-low. Grill 20 minutes. Brush, turn chicken on its side, and grill 10 minutes. Brush, and turn over onto the other side, and grill 10 minutes. Brush again, turn breast side up, and grill until the juices run clear and the chicken is white to the bone, about 15 to 20 minutes longer. The chicken should have grilled a total of about 1 hour and 20 minutes.

4. Remove and discard the lemon wedges. Present the chicken garnished with fresh lemon slices and sprigs of fresh sage if you have them. Carve the chicken or cut into quarters to serve.

All-American Barbecue Sauce

This is my favorite all-purpose barbecue sauce—much better than store-bought and so easy to make. If you cook up a big batch, extra sauce will keep in the refrigerator for at least two weeks.

Makes about 6 cups

¼ cup vegetable oil
1 large onion, chopped
3 garlic cloves, crushed in a press
1 tablespoon dry mustard
1½ teaspoons paprika
½ teaspoon cayenne
1½ cups ketchup

1½ cups bottled chili sauce
⅓ cup molasses
¼ cup Worcestershire sauce
¼ cup cider vinegar
2 bay leaves, broken in half
1½ cups beer (12 ounces)

1. Heat the oil in a medium nonaluminum saucepan. Add the onion and cook over medium heat, stirring, until the onion is softened, about 3 minutes.
2. Stir in the garlic, mustard, paprika, and cayenne. Cook 1 minute. Add all the remaining ingredients and bring to a boil. Reduce the heat to medium-low and simmer, stirring often, until lightly thickened, 20 to 25 minutes. Discard the bay leaves.

Jamaican Jerk Chicken

This spicy marinade can be applied to any part of the chicken that you prefer, even boneless breasts or thighs. It is also appropriate for pork, another popular "jerk" in Jamaica. Those with experience in hot peppers may well want to double the Scotch bonnets, but beware that these innocent-looking little veggies (and their jalapeño alternative) pack a very big punch!

4 Servings

⅓ cup olive oil
3 tablespoons distilled white vinegar
1½ tablespoons lime juice
1 tablespoon sugar
¼ cup minced scallions
2 garlic cloves, minced
1 Scotch bonnet or jalapeño pepper,
  seeded and minced

1 teaspoon dried thyme leaves
¾ teaspoon ground allspice
½ teaspoon cinnamon
½ teaspoon salt
¼ to ½ teaspoon cayenne, to taste
2½ to 3 pounds cut-up chicken

---

1. In a shallow dish large enough to hold the chicken in a single layer, combine the olive oil, vinegar, lime juice, sugar, scallions, garlic, minced pepper, thyme, allspice, cinnamon, salt, and cayenne. Add the chicken and turn to coat completely; then use your fingers to lift up the chicken skin and rub some of the marinade into the meat. Cover and refrigerate at least 4 hours or up to 24 hours. Return to room temperature before cooking.

2. Prepare a medium fire in a covered charcoal or gas grill. Grill the chicken, turning once or twice, until the outside is richly browned and the interior is no longer pink, with juices running clear when pierced with a knife tip, about 30 to 40 minutes. (White meat will take the lesser amount of time.)

West Coast Grilled Chicken Breasts

Today's style of cooking, long touted in avant-garde West Coast restaurants, favors lighter foods, lower in fat. Grilled skinless chicken breasts fill the bill quite nicely, especially when first marinated in this tangy mustard and lemon blend.

4 Servings

---

4 skinless, boneless chicken breast halves (about 5 ounces each)

1½ tablespoons olive oil

2 tablespoons lemon juice

1 tablespoon Dijon mustard

2 teaspoons white wine Worcestershire sauce

1 large garlic clove, minced

1 teaspoon grated lemon zest

¼ teaspoon crushed hot red pepper

---

1. Flatten the chicken breasts to an even thickness of about ¾ inch. In a shallow dish just large enough to hold the chicken in a single layer, combine the olive oil, lemon juice, mustard, Worcestershire, garlic, lemon zest, and hot pepper. Add the chicken and turn to coat evenly. Cover and refrigerate, turning often, for at least 1 hour and up to 6 hours.

2. Prepare a medium-hot fire in a covered charcoal or gas grill. Grill the chicken, turning once or twice and brushing often with the marinade, until the chicken is white throughout but still juicy, about 10 to 15 minutes.

Grilled Chicken "Cordon Bleu"

This is an American "gourmet" classic, updated and simplified for the grill. Serve it with a juicy vegetable, such as Grilled Ratatouille (p. 182) or stewed tomatoes, and a simple rice pilaf.

6 Servings

---

6 skinless, boneless chicken breasts (about 5 ounces each)
6 thin slices of Swiss or Gruyère cheese (about 3 ounces total)
6 thin slices of prosciutto (about 2 ounces total)

¾ cup Italian seasoned dry bread crumbs
3 tablespoons olive oil

---

1. Pound the chicken breasts between pieces of waxed paper to an even ¼-inch thickness. Layer a slice of cheese and prosciutto on each chicken breast, leaving a ¼-inch margin all around. Fold the chicken over to completely enclose the filling, then use your hands to form the chicken into a relatively even oval, smoothing the edges to seal. If necessary, the chicken can be secured with small skewers or soaked wooden toothpicks.

2. Put the bread crumbs on a plate. Brush the chicken with the olive oil, then dredge in the bread crumbs to coat completely. (The recipe can be prepared to this point up to 8 hours ahead and refrigerated.)

3. Prepare a medium-hot fire in a covered charcoal or gas grill. Grill the chicken, turning once with a spatula, until white in the center but still juicy, about 13 to 15 minutes total.

Texas Finger-Lickin' Barbecued Drumsticks

*Kids of all ages will love this sticky, sweet/hot sauce that is truly finger-lickin'
good, especially on juicy chicken drumsticks (and other chicken parts as well).
Because sauces of this type have a tendency to burn, brush on only during the
last 10 minutes or so of cooking time.*

8 Servings

---

1 tablespoon vegetable oil	1 cup chili sauce
1 small onion, chopped	⅓ cup molasses
1 tablespoon chili powder	⅓ cup cider vinegar
2 teaspoons dry mustard	16 chicken drumsticks (about 2½
½ teaspoon ground cumin	pounds)
½ teaspoon celery seeds, crushed	

---

1. In a medium saucepan, heat the oil, add the onion, and cook over medium
heat until just softened, about 3 minutes. Stir in the chili powder, mustard, cumin,
and celery seeds. Cook, stirring, for 1 minute. Stir in the chili sauce, molasses, and
vinegar. Lower the heat to medium-low and simmer 10 minutes, stirring often.
2. Prepare a medium-hot fire in a charcoal or gas grill. Grill the chicken for 20
minutes, turning occasionally. Brush with the sauce, then continue to grill, brushing
and turning often, until the chicken is white to the bone and richly browned and
crisp on the outside, about 10 to 15 minutes longer, for a total of 30 to 35 minutes.

Tandoori-Style Chicken with Cauliflower and Peppers

Indian tandoor, or clay oven cookery, produces food that is moist and tender, yet full of intense flavor. This is a delicious Americanized facsimile.

4 Servings

1 pound skinless, boneless chicken thighs	2 teaspoons ground cumin
	½ teaspoon ground turmeric
1 cup plain yogurt	½ teaspoon salt
1 tablespoon lemon juice	¼ teaspoon cayenne
1 tablespoon grated fresh ginger	2 cups cauliflower florets
2 garlic cloves, minced	1 red bell pepper, cut lengthwise into
2 teaspoons ground cardamom	8 thin wedges

1. Cut the chicken into 1- to 1½-inch chunks. In a mixing bowl, combine the yogurt, lemon juice, ginger, garlic, cardamom, cumin, turmeric, salt, and cayenne. Add the chicken and mix to coat completely. Cover and refrigerate at least 1 hour and up to 8 hours. Return to room temperature before cooking.

2. Cook the cauliflower in a large saucepan of boiling salted water just until crisp-tender, about 2 minutes. Rinse under cold water to cool; drain well.

3. Prepare a medium-hot fire in a covered charcoal or gas grill. Oil the grill rack. Remove the chicken from the marinade, but do not pat dry. Reserve the marinade. Thread the chicken, cauliflower, and red pepper wedges onto metal skewers. Brush the cauliflower and peppers with some of the marinade.

4. Grill, turning several times and brushing with any remaining marinade, until the chicken is white throughout but still juicy and the vegetables are lightly browned, about 12 to 14 minutes.

Skewered Basque Chicken

This is a rather free interpretation of a classic Basque chicken dish in which the chicken and vegetables are usually cooked with rice in a frying pan, much like a paella. Here, the bright peppers, onions, and tomatoes are skewered with chunks of flavorful dark-meat chicken, then served over a rice pilaf studded with olives and parsley. The grilled taste of the chicken and vegetables is just right in this rustic dish.

6 Servings

⅓ cup dry red wine

¼ cup olive oil

2 tablespoons sherry wine vinegar

4 garlic cloves, chopped

½ teaspoon salt

¼ teaspoon crushed hot red pepper

1½ pounds skinless, boneless chicken thighs

6 ounces smoked ham, cut in 1 thick piece

1 large red onion

1 green bell pepper

1 yellow bell pepper

12 cherry tomatoes

6 cups hot cooked white rice

½ cup chopped pimiento-stuffed olives

½ cup chopped parsley

3 or 4 handfuls grapevine cuttings, optional

---

1. In a shallow dish just large enough to hold the chicken, combine the wine, olive oil, vinegar, garlic, salt, and hot pepper. Cut the chicken into 1½-inch chunks and add to the marinade; turn to coat evenly. Cover and refrigerate at least 1 hour and up to 4 hours.

2. Prepare a hot fire in a covered charcoal or gas grill. If using grapevine cuttings, soak them in cold water for at least 30 minutes. Cut the ham into 1-inch chunks, and the onion and green and yellow peppers into 1½-inch chunks. Thread the chicken, ham, and all of the vegetables onto 6 metal skewers, alternating the ingredients and placing the tomatoes at both ends of the skewers. Brush all of the ingredients with some of the chicken marinade.

3. Just before cooking, toss the grapevine cuttings onto the coals. Grill the skewered meat and vegetables, turning occasionally and brushing with the marinade, until the chicken is just cooked through, the ham is browned, and the vegetables are tender, about 12 to 14 minutes.

4. Stir together the rice, olives, and parsley. Arrange the skewers atop the rice.

Grilled Chicken Patties Provençal

Ground chicken is increasingly available in most supermarkets. If you can't find it, grind your own from boneless chicken breasts: Cut the chicken into chunks, then pulse them in a food processor until coarsely ground. Or use ground turkey. These patties are seasoned with the sunny herbs of the Mediterranean, then grilled and served on garlicky toasts for an open-faced sandwich that is irresistible.

6 Servings

1 egg
1½ pounds ground chicken or turkey
⅔ cup fresh white bread crumbs
¼ cup chopped parsley, preferably flat leaf
3 tablespoons chopped fresh basil or 1 tablespoon dried
1 tablespoon chopped fresh marjoram or 1 teaspoon dried

½ teaspoon salt
¼ teaspoon freshly ground pepper
⅛ teaspoon cayenne
¼ cup mayonnaise
1 garlic clove, crushed through a press
6 slices of French bread, cut diagonally about ½ inch thick
1 small bunch of arugula, pulled apart
6 thin slices of tomato

1. Prepare a medium-hot fire in a covered charcoal or gas grill. Oil the grill rack.
2. In a medium bowl, beat the egg lightly. Add the chicken, bread crumbs, parsley, chopped basil, marjoram, salt, pepper, and cayenne. Use your hands to blend well. Form into 6 patties, each about 3 inches in diameter. In a small bowl, mix together the mayonnaise and garlic. Lightly brush both sides of each bread slice with some of the garlic mayonnaise.
3. Grill the chicken patties, turning once, until they are white throughout but still juicy, about 13 to 16 minutes. A few minutes before the chicken is done, set the

bread at the sides of the grill and cook, turning once, until lightly toasted, about 2 minutes total.

4. To assemble, brush one side of the toasts with half of the remaining garlic mayonnaise. Place, mayonnaise side up, on a plate and cover with arugula leaves, tomato, and chicken patties in that order. Brush the tops of the warm chicken patties with the remaining garlic mayonnaise.

Grilled Vietnamese Chicken Noodle Salad

The marinade also doubles as the dressing in this easy, Vietnamese-inspired main dish salad. Fish sauce, a widely used Thai and Vietnamese ingredient, is available at Asian markets and in many large supermarkets.

4 Servings

¼ cup fish sauce (*nam pla*)
¼ cup lime juice
1 tablespoon soy sauce
¼ cup chopped fresh mint, plus sprigs for garnish
3 garlic cloves, chopped
2 jalapeño peppers, finely chopped
1 teaspoon sugar
¼ cup plus 2 tablespoons olive oil

4 skinless, boneless chicken breast halves (about 5 ounces each)
1 small red bell pepper, quartered
1 small yellow bell pepper, quartered
8 whole scallions, trimmed
8 ounces thin Asian noodles or vermicelli, cooked and drained
½ cup coarsely chopped unsalted peanuts

---

1. In a small mixing bowl, whisk together the fish sauce, lime juice, soy sauce, chopped mint, garlic, jalapeño peppers, and sugar. Whisk in the olive oil. Pour about ⅓ of the marinade into a shallow dish just large enough to hold the chicken, reserving the remainder to use as a dressing. Use your hands to flatten the chicken to an even thickness, then place in the marinade and turn to coat both sides. Cover and refrigerate, turning occasionally, at least 1 hour and up to 4 hours.
2. Prepare a medium-hot fire in a covered charcoal or gas grill. Remove the chicken from the marinade and add the peppers and scallions to the marinade; turn to coat. Grill the chicken and peppers, turning occasionally, until the chicken is white throughout but still juicy and the peppers are lightly browned and softened, about 8 to 10 minutes. Add the scallions to the grill during the last few minutes

---

of cooking time, and grill, turning once or twice, until lightly browned and softened, about 3 to 5 minutes.

3. Cut the grilled pepper quarters into thin strips and the scallions into ¾-inch lengths. Toss the vegetables and the hot pasta with the reserved dressing. Place on a large serving platter or individual plates. Cut the chicken into crosswise slices and arrange decoratively atop the noodles. Sprinkle with the chopped peanuts and garnish with the mint sprigs.

Grilled Caesar's Chicken Salad

6 Servings

½ cup plus 2 tablespoons extra-virgin olive oil

2 garlic cloves, crushed through a press

3 tablespoons lemon juice

2 tablespoons red wine vinegar

1 teaspoon Dijon mustard

½ teaspoon freshly ground pepper

6 skinless, boneless chicken breasts (about 5 ounces each)

1 (2-ounce) can flat anchovies, drained and chopped

4 French bread slices, cut diagonally ½ inch thick

1 large head of romaine lettuce, leaves torn

¼ cup grated Parmesan cheese

1. In a small dish, stir together the olive oil and the garlic. Let stand 15 minutes. Reserve 2 tablespoons of the garlic oil, whisk the remainder with the lemon juice, vinegar, mustard, and pepper. Use your hands to flatten the chicken to an even thickness and place the chicken in a shallow dish. Pour ¼ cup of the vinaigrette over the chicken; turn to coat both sides. Let stand 20 minutes. Stir the anchovies into the remaining vinaigrette.

2. Prepare a hot fire in a covered charcoal or gas grill. Grill the chicken, turning once, until white throughout but still juicy, about 8 to 10 minutes. About 3 minutes before the chicken is done, brush both sides of the bread with the reserved garlic oil and set at the edge of the grill, turning once to lightly toast both sides.

3. In a large bowl, toss the romaine lettuce with the anchovy vinaigrette. Add the cheese and toss again. Divide among 6 serving plates. Slice the chicken crosswise and arrange the chicken on top of the lettuce. Set a grilled crouton on each salad plate.

Grilled Turkey Sausage Pasta Salad

This hot pasta salad is a fabulous summer whole meal in one. I like the salad made with the long, squiggly spirals called fusilli, but almost any sturdy pasta shape works well here. These days, good bottled low-fat or fat-free Italian dressings are available in supermarkets. This is a fine use for them.

4 Servings

---

1 pound Italian-seasoned turkey sausage

1 red bell pepper, quartered

1 green bell pepper, quartered

1 bunch of scallions, trimmed

1 cup bottled low-fat or fat-free Italian vinaigrette salad dressing

1 pound fusilli or other sturdy pasta

¼ cup grated Parmesan cheese

¼ cup sliced black olives

---

1. Prepare a medium-hot fire in a covered charcoal or gas grill. Oil the grill rack. Prick each sausage in several places. Brush both peppers and the scallions with some of the salad dressing. Grill the sausage, turning often, until browned and no trace of pink remains, about 12 to 15 minutes. Grill the peppers, turning often, until softened and lightly browned, about 10 to 12 minutes. Grill the scallions, turning often, until softened and lightly browned, about 5 to 7 minutes.

2. Meanwhile, in a large pot of boiling salted water, cook the pasta until tender but still firm, 10 to 12 minutes; drain. Cut the sausage into 1-inch chunks, the peppers into thin strips, and the scallions into ½-inch slices.

3. Toss the sausage, peppers, and scallions with the pasta and the remaining salad dressing. Add the cheese and olives and toss again. Serve hot or at room temperature.

Grill-Smoked Turkey with Peppered Peach Glaze

Small hen turkeys or capons are the best size for conventional grilling. It is important to keep the coals at medium and have the turkey set away from the direct heat so that the bird will cook through to a tender smokiness before the skin is charred. Brush with the peppered peach sauce, or any other sauce that you will be using, only during the last half hour or so of cooking to prevent burning. The result is a wonderful variation on roast turkey.

8 Servings

---

1 cup peach preserves
1 cup dry white wine
2 tablespoons vegetable oil
¾ teaspoon freshly ground pepper
2 tablespoons chopped fresh ginger or
   1 teaspoon ground ginger

1 small whole turkey or capon, 7 to 9
   pounds
Salt
¼ cup water

5 or 6 handfuls mesquite wood chips

---

1. In a small saucepan, heat the preserves, ½ cup of the wine, 1 tablespoon of the oil, the ¾ teaspoon pepper, and the ginger over medium-low heat, stirring occasionally, until the preserves melt, about 5 minutes. Remove from the heat and let cool.

2. Remove the giblets from the turkey; discard or reserve for another use. Rinse the turkey inside and out and pat it dry. Rub the skin of the turkey with the remaining 1 tablespoon oil. Season liberally inside and out with salt and additional pepper.

3. Prepare a medium fire in a covered charcoal or gas grill, leaving the grate off the charcoal grill. If using coals, push them to one side when they are ready. Oil the grill rack and set it on the grill. Soak the wood chips in cold water for at least 30 minutes.

4. Place an aluminum foil drip pan opposite the coals and fill the pan with the remaining ½ cup wine and ¼ cup of water. Toss about half of the wet wood chips onto the hot coals or add to a gas grill according to the manufacturer's directions.

5. Set the turkey, breast side down, on the rack over the drip pan if there is one. Cook 20 minutes, rotate the bird 90 degrees, and cook 20 minutes. If using a gas grill, reduce the heat to medium-low. Turn breast side up and cook 20 minutes. Rotate another 90 degrees and cook 20 minutes. Turn the turkey breast side up again and cook 20 minutes. Toss the remaining wet wood chips onto the coals.

6. Brush the turkey all over with the sauce and continue to cook, breast side up, brushing every 10 minutes with the sauce, until the internal temperature registers 170 degrees on an instant-reading thermometer, about 40 to 50 minutes longer. (The turkey will cook a total of about 2 hours.) Let the turkey rest for 15 minutes before carving.

Summer Herb-Stuffed Grilled Turkey Breast

Turkey breast halves are easier and quicker to cook than the whole breast. So if you want to serve more people, simply double this recipe and cook 2 halves. Stuffing the fresh herbs under the skin not only looks pretty but infuses the meat with more flavor than simply brushing or marinating can impart. You can use a combination of almost any fresh herbs in your garden or from the produce stand, but I particularly like this easy-to-grow trio.

4 Servings

1 turkey breast half with back and rib portions, 2 to 2½ pounds

⅓ cup loosely packed chopped fresh summer savory

⅓ cup loosely packed chopped fresh chives

⅓ cup loosely packed chopped flat-leaf parsley

2 tablespoons olive oil

2 tablespoons white wine vinegar

2 garlic cloves, finely chopped

½ teaspoon salt

¼ teaspoon freshly ground pepper

1 cup additional herb sprigs, optional

1. Use your fingers to loosen the skin on the turkey breast, separating it from the meat without tearing the skin. Insert half of the chopped savory, chives, and parsley under the skin. Place the turkey breast in a shallow dish.

2. In a small bowl, combine the remaining chopped herbs with the olive oil, vinegar, garlic, salt, and pepper. Brush the marinade all over the turkey breast. Refrigerate at least 4 hours and up to 24 hours.

3. Prepare a medium fire in a charcoal grill; use tongs to push the coals to one side when they are ready. Set a drip pan with about ½ inch water and the optional extra herb sprigs opposite the coals. Or prepare an indirect fire in a gas grill according to the manufacturer's directions.

4. Set the turkey on the rack over the drip pan and grill, turning once or twice and brushing with any remaining marinade, until the meat is white to the bone and the internal temperature registers 170 degrees on an instant-reading thermometer, about 50 to 60 minutes. Let the turkey rest for 10 minutes before carving into slices.

Mahogany Turkey Legs

If the drumstick is your favorite part of the turkey, then this is your recipe, though the glaze is just as good on a whole bird, or on the breast, or on the thighs, or even on chicken, for that matter. Mesquite wood chips give even more dimension to the taste.

4 Servings

¼ cup molasses
¼ cup cider vinegar
1 tablespoon Worcestershire sauce
1 tablespoon vegetable oil
1 tablespoon Dijon mustard

½ teaspoon freshly ground pepper
2 turkey drumsticks (about 2½ pounds total)

4 to 6 handfuls mesquite wood chips

---

1. In a small saucepan, heat the molasses, vinegar, Worcestershire sauce, oil, mustard, and pepper just to a simmer. Remove from the heat and let cool.

2. Prepare a medium fire in a charcoal grill; use tongs to push the coals to one side when they are ready to cook. Place an aluminum foil drip pan on the side opposite the coals. Or prepare an indirect fire in a gas grill according to the manufacturer's directions. Oil the grill rack. Soak the wood chips in water for at least 30 minutes.

3. Toss half of the wet chips onto the hot coals or add to a gas grill according to the manufacturer's directions. Set the turkey legs on the grill over the drip pan. Grill 10 minutes per side, then brush with some of the molasses glaze. Continue to grill, turning and brushing often with the glaze, until the turkey drumsticks are richly browned, the skin is crisp, and the meat is cooked to the bone, an additional 1 to 1¼ hours, tossing the remaining wet wood chips onto the coals about halfway through the cooking time.

Grilled Turkey Taco Salad

This taco salad is a pleasant change of pace from the usual ground beef mix and is an easy, colorful summer supper that the whole family will love. You can use chicken breasts or boneless thighs in place of turkey if you wish.

4 Servings

1 pound boneless turkey breast fillets
1 tablespoon chili powder
½ teaspoon salt
¼ teaspoon cayenne
¼ cup vegetable or corn oil
2 tablespoons red wine vinegar
½ teaspoon ground cumin
1 small head of green leaf lettuce, torn up

1 small head of red leaf lettuce, torn up
1 cup bottled salsa, hot or medium
4 ounces shredded Monterey Jack cheese (about 1 cup)
4 cups corn tortilla chips

1. Season the turkey with the chili powder and half each of the salt and cayenne. Let stand 30 minutes. In a small bowl, whisk together the oil, vinegar, cumin, and remaining salt and cayenne.

2. Prepare a hot fire in a covered charcoal or gas grill. Oil the grill rack. Grill the turkey, turning once, until white throughout but still juicy, about 5 to 6 minutes total.

3. In a large shallow bowl, toss together the vinaigrette and the green and red leaf lettuce. Thinly slice the turkey and arrange over the center of the greens. Spoon some of the salsa in a strip over the turkey slices. Sprinkle the cheese and the chips around the edges of the salad.

Thanksgiving in July Turkey Burgers

If the Fourth of July isn't a day of thanksgiving, then I'm not sure what is! So, why not combine the burgers of summer with the flavors of late November? These turkey burgers are seasoned with crushed cornbread stuffing, then served on rolls with an instant homemade cranberry ketchup.

6 Servings

½ cup finely chopped celery
½ cup finely chopped onion
1 tablespoon vegetable oil or butter
1 teaspoon poultry seasoning
1 egg, beaten
1½ pounds ground turkey or chicken
½ cup crushed seasoned packaged corn-
    bread stuffing

½ teaspoon salt
¼ teaspoon freshly ground pepper
6 sandwich rolls, preferably potato rolls
1 cup Cranberry Ketchup (recipe
    follows)

1. Prepare a medium-hot fire in a covered charcoal or gas grill. Oil the grill rack.
2. In a medium frying pan, cook the celery and onion in the oil over medium heat, stirring often, until the vegetables are softened, about 3 minutes. Stir in the poultry seasoning. Remove from the heat and let cool.
3. In a mixing bowl, use your hands to combine the egg, turkey, stuffing crumbs, salt, pepper, and cooked onions and celery. Form into 6 patties, each about 3 inches in diameter.
4. Grill the turkey patties, turning once until they are white throughout but still juicy, about 13 to 16 minutes. About 2 minutes before the burgers are done, toast the cut sides of the rolls lightly at the edge of the grill.
5. Assemble the burgers on the toasted rolls. Serve with Cranberry Ketchup.

Cranberry Ketchup

This tangy condiment is great on turkey burgers, turkey franks, and on grilled turkey cutlets.

Makes about 1 cup

---

1 cup canned whole berry cranberry sauce

2 tablespoons freshly grated or prepared white horseradish

2 teaspoons lemon juice

Salt and freshly ground pepper

---

1. In a small bowl, combine the cranberry sauce, horseradish, and lemon juice. Stir to blend well. Season with salt and pepper to taste.

2. Let stand at least 15 minutes or refrigerate up to 5 days before using.

Grilled Game Hens with Mango Salsa

4 Servings

2 whole Cornish game hens, halved
  (about 1¼ pounds each)
1½ teaspoons paprika
1½ teaspoons dried oregano
1½ teaspoons dried thyme leaves
½ teaspoon cayenne
½ teaspoon salt
¼ teaspoon freshly ground pepper

2 tablespoons vegetable oil
1 large garlic clove, minced
1 large mango, coarsely chopped
¼ cup finely chopped red onion
1 small jalapeño pepper, seeded and
  minced
2 tablespoons chopped fresh cilantro
1 tablespoon lime juice

1. Use your hands to flatten the hen halves for even cooking. With your fingers loosen the skin to separate it from the meat without tearing it. In a small dish, mix together the paprika, oregano, thyme, cayenne, salt, and pepper. Rub this spice mixture under the skin of the hens. In another small dish, combine the oil and garlic. Brush the hens all over with the oil mixture. Let the hens stand about 30 minutes or cover and refrigerate up to 8 hours. Return to room temperature before cooking.

2. For the salsa, in a small bowl, combine the chopped mango, red onion, jalapeño pepper, cilantro, and lime juice. Stir to mix well. Let stand 15 minutes or cover and refrigerate up to 4 hours, but return to room temperature to serve.

3. Prepare a medium fire in a covered charcoal or gas grill. Grill the hen halves, turning once, until the skin is richly browned and the juices run clear when pricked with a knife tip, about 30 to 40 minutes. Serve the hens warm with the room-temperature salsa.

Grilled Crabapple- and Sage-Glazed Quail

Quail are tiny dark-meated birds that make a sophisticated presentation, but are quick and easy to cook. Wild rice studded with walnuts and a colorful radicchio salad would make this a fabulous end-of-summer party. If you have a friendly butcher, he or she will probably butterfly the quail for you.

6 Servings

12 quail (3 to 4 ounces each)	1 tablespoon Worcestershire sauce
½ cup crabapple or apple jelly	1 tablespoon olive oil
2 tablespoons dry white wine	¾ teaspoon salt
1 tablespoon chopped fresh sage or 1 teaspoon dried	½ teaspoon freshly ground pepper

1. Rinse the quail under cold water and pat dry. Use a cleaver or poultry shears to cut through the backbone of each bird. Place the quail, skin side up, on a work surface and flatten with the palm of your hand to butterfly the birds.

2. In a shallow dish just large enough to hold the quail in a single layer, combine all of the remaining ingredients. Add the quail, turning to coat completely. Cover and refrigerate at least 4 hours or up to 12 hours. Return to room temperature before cooking.

3. Prepare a hot fire in a charcoal or gas grill. Grill the quail, skin side down, for 5 minutes. Brush with some of the marinade, turn, and grill until the skin is nicely browned and the meat is barely pink and juicy, about 5 minutes longer.

Grilled Duck Breast with Nectarine-Mint Salsa

Duck and fruit are a natural pairing. This is a contemporary interpretation of the classic culinary marriage. Boned duck breasts are increasingly available at meat markets, so ask your butcher. The salsa is excellent with grilled game hens, too.

6 Servings

3 whole duck breasts, boned, skinned, and split in half (about 1½ pounds total meat)
¼ cup lime juice
2 tablespoons olive oil
¾ teaspoon salt
½ teaspoon freshly ground pepper

1 pound ripe but firm nectarines (about 4), coarsely chopped
⅔ cup finely chopped red onion
1 jalapeño pepper, minced
⅓ cup chopped fresh mint, plus sprigs for garnish

1. Rinse the duck breasts with cold water and pat dry. In a shallow dish just large enough to hold the duck, stir together 1 tablespoon of the lime juice with the olive oil, ¼ teaspoon salt, and ¼ teaspoon pepper. Add the duck and turn to coat. Let stand 15 minutes or refrigerate up to 4 hours. Return to room temperature before cooking.

2. In a mixing bowl, combine the chopped nectarines, red onion, jalapeño pepper, remaining 3 tablespoons lime juice, and remaining salt and pepper. Stir to mix well. Let stand 15 minutes or refrigerate up to 4 hours. About 10 minutes before serving, stir the chopped mint into the salsa.

3. Prepare a hot fire in a covered charcoal or gas grill. Grill the duck, turning once, until browned and cooked through, 8 to 10 minutes. Serve the duck topped with the salsa and garnished with mint sprigs.

Chapter Three
Beef, Veal, and Venison

Beef, from burgers to T-bones, is the quintessential stuff of grilling. Its intrinsic heartiness makes beef an excellent candidate for aromatic woods, such as hickory and mesquite. In fact, these woods tend to bring out the best flavor of beef; they also add natural accents to venison and other game.

Marinades, though used in all types of grill cookery, are particularly well suited to beef and game. In years past, marinades were especially useful since the relatively high acid content (usually from vinegar) helped to tenderize and preserve the tough old meat. These days, we have fairly tender meat to begin with, and marinate meats for much shorter periods of time, but the wonderful flavors of both traditional and innovative marinades do permeate the meat, especially in thin cuts such as steak.

If using a marinade, prepare it in a shallow, nonreactive dish or pan just big enough to hold the meat comfortably. Then be sure to turn the meat in the marinade so that the flavor will permeate all surfaces evenly. Very thin cuts can be marinated an hour or so at room temperature, but roasts should stand longer, even up to 2 days, in the refrigerator. Just remember to turn the meat in the liquid every couple of hours and let it return to room temperature before cooking.

When grilling, follow your own preferences for desired degree of doneness. Tender cuts, such as filet mignon, take well to shorter cooking over higher heat, but briskets and other tougher cuts are best with a little longer time over lower coals. All cuts of veal should be treated like tender beef.

A little practice with your own grill will perfect your ability to judge the timing for a rare, medium, or well-done steak. It is both easier to cook and better tasting to use thicker (about 1 inch or more) rather than thinner steaks, which tend to dry out. For larger cuts, an instant-reading thermometer is better than cutting into the meat, which causes juices to be lost. Let steaks and roasts stand for about 10 minutes before carving. During this time, the meat continues to cook a bit. A good trick is to take it off the grill just a minute or two before it is done to your liking, so that it will not overcook.

Grilled Steak Au Poivre with Caramelized Leeks

Filet mignon is my first choice for this elegant yet simple main course, but other tender beef steaks such as rib-eye or strip steaks are tasty, too. Because of their natural sugar content, leeks caramelize nicely on the grill and make a succulent juxtaposition with the peppery beef. If you can't find slender leeks, use thick scallions instead.

6 Servings

---

6 filet mignon steaks, cut 1 inch thick (about 5 ounces each)

Salt

1 tablespoon cracked black peppercorns

6 slender leeks, each ¾ to 1 inch in diameter

1 tablespoon olive oil

½ teaspoon dried thyme leaves

---

1. Prepare a hot fire in a covered charcoal or gas grill. Season the meat lightly with salt, then pat the pepper firmly onto both sides of the steaks. Trim the leeks to include 1 inch of the pale green parts. Cut the leeks in half lengthwise. Rinse very well; dry with paper towels. Brush the leeks with the olive oil, then sprinkle with the thyme.

2. Grill the meat, turning once, 3 to 4 minutes per side for rare to medium-rare, or longer to desired degree of doneness. Grill the leeks at the sides of the grill, turning 2 or 3 times, until softened and golden brown on the outside, about 8 minutes.

3. Serve the meat with the leeks crisscrossed over the top.

Teriyaki Flank Steak with Grilled Shiitake Mushrooms

6 Servings

⅓ cup soy sauce
¼ cup dry sherry
3 tablespoons vegetable oil
⅓ cup chopped scallions, plus 12
   whole scallions

2 garlic cloves, chopped
1½ pounds flank steak
12 shiitake mushrooms, stemmed

1. In a shallow dish just large enough to hold the meat, combine the soy sauce, sherry, oil, chopped scallions, and garlic. Add the flank steak and turn to coat both sides. Cover and refrigerate at least 6 hours and up to 24 hours, turning occasionally.
2. Prepare a hot fire in a covered charcoal or gas grill. Remove the meat from the marinade and pat it dry with paper towels. Trim the whole scallions, leaving 2 inches of the green part. Toss the scallions and mushrooms in the marinade to coat, then thread them onto metal skewers.
3. Grill the meat, turning once, to desired degree of doneness, 12 to 15 minutes for rare, 15 to 18 minutes for medium-rare to medium. Let the meat rest for 5 minutes before slicing thinly across the grain.
4. Meanwhile, grill the skewered scallions and mushrooms at the edge, or cooler part of the grill, turning once, until softened and the edges are browned, about 2 to 4 minutes.
5. Arrange the meat on a serving platter. Place the grilled scallions and mushrooms on top, and serve.

Zesty Orange Beef Sticks

The flavors here, borrowed from several exotic cuisines, are at once sweet and sour, cooling and hot, and thoroughly delightful. Serve atop a simple rice pilaf.

6 Servings

1½ pounds sirloin or top round steak
3 navel oranges
3 tablespoons cider vinegar
1 tablespoon molasses
1 tablespoon vegetable oil

2 garlic cloves, minced
3 tablespoons chopped cilantro or parsley
¼ to ½ teaspoon crushed hot red pepper, to taste

1. Cut the beef across the grain into ¼-inch-thick slices. (This is easier to do if the meat is partially frozen.) Use a sharp knife to peel off the skin from the oranges in large pieces or in a spiral. Be sure to cut only the colored zest of the peel and avoid the white pith, which is bitter.

2. Squeeze the juice from the oranges into a shallow dish large enough to hold the meat. Stir in the vinegar, molasses, oil, garlic, cilantro, orange peel, and hot pepper. Add the beef and turn to coat with the marinade. Cover and refrigerate at least 2 hours and up to 8 hours. Return to room temperature before cooking.

3. Prepare a hot fire in a covered charcoal or gas grill. Thread the beef and orange zest strips alternating onto 6 metal skewers. Grill 3 to 4 minutes per side, brushing once or twice with the marinade, until the meat is medium-rare and the orange peels are tinged with brown. Serve from the skewers.

Steak Fajitas

I first tasted fajitas, using the skirt steaks so popular in the Southwest, as street food while living in San Antonio in the late sixties. Since then, this regional specialty has become an American fixture. Though they can be fancied up as much as you wish, they are really quite simple to make, especially if you use some of the excellent prepared salsas on the market today.

4 Servings

---

1 pound sirloin steak, cut ½ to ¾ inch thick, or skirt steak or flank steak

Salt and freshly ground pepper

2 tablespoons lime juice

1½ tablespoons vegetable oil

1 small jalapeño pepper, seeded and minced

8 (7- or 8-inch) flour tortillas

1 cup Simple Guacamole (recipe follows)

1 cup shredded Monterey Jack cheese

1 cup bottled or fresh salsa

---

1. Season the steak lightly with salt and pepper. In a shallow dish just large enough to accommodate the meat, combine the lime juice, oil, and jalapeño pepper. Add the steak and turn to coat it completely. Let the meat stand at room temperature, turning once or twice, for 30 minutes. If using flank steak, marinate in the refrigerator for 2 to 4 hours. Wrap the tortillas together in aluminum foil.

2. Prepare a hot fire in a covered charcoal or gas grill. Set the tortillas at the edge of the grill to warm. Grill the meat until rare to medium-rare, 3 to 4 minutes per side for sirloin, 2 to 3 for skirt, or 5 to 7 for flank steak. Remove the meat to a cutting board and thinly slice against the grain.

3. To assemble the fajitas, spread one side of each warmed tortilla with some of the guacamole. Divide the meat and accumulated juices among the tortillas, then top with the cheese and salsa. Roll or fold up the tortillas to enclose the filling.

Simple Guacamole

I prefer the black, wrinkled Hass avocado from California, but a ripe green Florida avocado makes a good guacamole, too. Ripe avocados yield to pressure, but are not mushy. They are normally rock-hard in the grocery store, but they will ripen nicely on the counter in a couple of days.

Makes about 1 cup

---

1 large ripe avocado, halved and pitted
2 tablespoons plain yogurt or sour
   cream

1 tablespoon lime juice
2 dashes of Tabasco sauce
Salt and freshly ground pepper

---

1. Scoop out the avocado and place it in a mixing bowl. Mash the avocado with the yogurt, lime juice, and Tabasco to make a coarse puree. Season with salt and pepper to taste.
2. Use the guacamole immediately, or cover with plastic wrap pressed directly on its surface and refrigerate up to 2 hours.

Thai Grilled Beef Salad

Asian beef salads are a really hot item on trendy menus these days. This version is easy to make at home, since it uses readily available ingredients.

4 Servings

½ cup peanut oil
¼ cup lime juice
¼ cup finely chopped fresh basil
¼ cup finely chopped scallions
¼ cup finely chopped fresh mint
2 garlic cloves, minced
1½ teaspoons grated fresh ginger
1 teaspoon finely chopped jalapeño
    pepper

1 pound flank steak
6 cups shredded iceberg lettuce
1 cucumber, seeded and thinly sliced
8 small radishes
8 small cherry tomatoes
¼ cup chopped salted peanuts

1. In a small bowl, combine the peanut oil, lime juice, basil, scallions, mint, garlic, ginger, and jalapeño pepper. Pour half of the marinade into a shallow dish just large enough to hold the steak. Add the meat and turn to coat. Cover and refrigerate the meat for at least 6 hours and up to 24 hours, turning occasionally. Reserve the remaining marinade to use as a salad dressing.
2. Prepare a medium-hot fire in a covered charcoal or gas grill. Grill the meat rare to medium-rare, a total of 12 to 15 minutes, brushing often with the marinade left in the dish and turning once. Let the meat rest for 5 minutes, then slice thinly across the grain.

3. Arrange the lettuce on serving plates, then place the cucumber, radishes, and tomatoes around the edges of the plates. Arrange the steak in the center of the salads and drizzle any juices from the carving board over the meat. Spoon the reserved marinade/dressing over the salads and sprinkle the peanuts on top.

Grilled Beef Tenderloin with a Trio of Sauces

This may just be the ultimate party dish, certainly worthy its trio of sauces, especially since each is so amazingly easy to make. All are served at room temperature. Have the butcher trim and tie the meat for you. An instant-reading thermometer is a big help to be sure that the meat does not overcook.

10 to 12 Servings

1 cup mayonnaise
¼ cup grainy Dijon mustard
1 cup packed watercress sprigs
1 garlic clove, minced
1 tablespoon lemon juice
¾ cup sour cream or plain yogurt
3 tablespoons prepared white
  horseradish

Salt and freshly ground pepper
1 whole beef tenderloin, trimmed and
  tied (about 5 pounds total)
1 tablespoon olive oil
2 teaspoons coarsely ground black
  pepper
1 teaspoon salt

1. In a small dish, blend together ½ cup of the mayonnaise with the mustard. In a food processor, finely chop the watercress. In another small dish, combine the chopped watercress with the remaining ½ cup mayonnaise, garlic, and lemon juice. In a third small dish, combine the sour cream with the horseradish. Season all three sauces with salt and freshly ground pepper to taste. Cover each and refrigerate up to 8 hours, but return to room temperature to serve.
2. Prepare a medium-hot fire in a covered charcoal or gas grill. Brush the meat with the olive oil, then sprinkle with the 2 teaspoons coarsely ground pepper and 1 teaspoon salt, patting so the seasonings will adhere.

3. Grill the meat, turning occasionally, until the outside is well browned and inside is cooked to the desired degree of doneness, 25 to 30 minutes for rare, 30 to 35 minutes for medium-rare; an instant-reading thermometer will register 130 to 140 degrees.

4. Let the meat rest for 10 minutes before carving. Serve accompanied by the three sauces.

Grill-Smoked Brisket with Chuck Wagon Barbecue Sauce

If you have a smoker, follow the directions for Hotter 'n Hell Smoked Beef Brisket (p. 198), but if you are using a covered grill, this is the best way to cook brisket. The preliminary roasting in the oven seals in the juices and intensifies the flavor, and the time on the grill gives the meat that great crisped edge that is so prized among brisket lovers. The extra bonus is that the first part of the cooking can be done several hours or even a day ahead, which makes this a fine recipe for entertaining.

8 to 10 Servings

---

2 tablespoons chili powder
1 tablespoon paprika
1 teaspoon garlic powder
1 teaspoon dried oregano
1 teaspoon salt
¼ teaspoon cayenne

1 whole beef brisket, well trimmed
   (5 to 6 pounds)
3 to 4 cups Chuck Wagon Barbecue
   Sauce (recipe follows)

3 to 4 handfuls hickory chips

---

1. In a small dish, mix together the chili powder, paprika, garlic powder, oregano, salt, and cayenne. Rub the seasoning mix all over the brisket. Wrap the brisket tightly in heavy-duty aluminum foil.

2. Preheat the oven to 325 degrees. Place the meat on a rack set in a baking pan over about ¼ inch of water. Bake 3 to 4 hours, or until the meat is very tender. (The recipe can be prepared to this point a day ahead, cooled, and refrigerated in the foil. Return to room temperature before continuing.)

3. Soak the wood chips in cold water for at least 30 minutes. Prepare a medium-hot fire in a covered charcoal or gas grill. Remove the meat from the foil. Just before cooking, toss the wet hickory chips directly onto the hot coals or add to a gas grill according to the manufacturer's instructions. Grill, turning once or twice, until the meat is richly browned on both sides and heated through, about 20 to 30 minutes. Meanwhile, heat the barbecue sauce to a simmer in a saucepan.

4. Let the meat stand for about 10 minutes, then thinly slice across the grain. Mix the meat with about half of the barbecue sauce. Serve the remaining sauce on the side. (Leftover brisket can be refrigerated in the sauce, then reheated, covered, in a 325 degree oven for about 30 minutes until hot. Some people think it is even better than the first time around.)

Chuck Wagon Barbecue Sauce

This is a somewhat chunky sauce that is especially good with brisket, but it is also tasty with barbecued pork roasts.

Makes about 4 cups

3 tablespoons vegetable oil	1 (14½- to 16-ounce) can tomatoes,
1 onion, chopped	with juices
1 green bell pepper, chopped	1 cup bottled chili sauce
1 celery rib, chopped	1 cup beer
2 garlic cloves, crushed through a	2 tablespoons prepared white
press	horseradish
¼ cup chili powder	2 tablespoons cider vinegar
1½ teaspoons dry mustard	2 tablespoons Worcestershire sauce

(continued on next page)

(continued from previous page)

1. Heat the oil in a large nonaluminum saucepan. Add the onion, green pepper, and celery and cook over medium heat for 3 minutes, or until softened. Add the garlic and cook 1 minute. Stir in the chili powder and mustard and cook, stirring, for 1 minute. Stir in the tomatoes with their juices, the chili sauce, beer, horseradish, vinegar, and Worcestershire. With the back of a spoon, break up the tomatoes. Simmer, stirring occasionally, until reduced by about one-fourth, 25 to 30 minutes.
2. Use immediately, or cover and refrigerate up to 2 weeks.

Grill-Smoked Country Chuck Roast

This is definitely not grandmother's pot roast, but it may become the new standard at your house. The combination of direct grilling and foil-wrapped "roasting" results in fork-tender, lightly smoky meat that is a cross between Sunday dinner and Saturday night barbecue.

8 Servings

---

1 cup dry red wine
½ cup red wine vinegar
2 tablespoons vegetable oil
2 cups thinly sliced onions
2 large garlic cloves, minced
1 tablespoon cracked black peppercorns
1 teaspoon salt

1½ teaspoons dried thyme leaves
1½ teaspoons dried oregano
1 teaspoon celery seeds
3½ to 4 pounds boneless chuck roast,
    about 2 inches thick, well trimmed
4 carrots, sliced

---

1. In a large bowl, combine the wine, vinegar, oil, onions, garlic, peppercorns, salt, thyme, oregano, and celery seeds. Add the meat and turn to coat completely. Cover and refrigerate at least 8 hours and up to 48 hours, turning occasionally. Return to room temperature before grilling.

2. Prepare a medium-hot fire in a covered charcoal or gas grill. Remove the meat from the marinade and reserve the marinade. Grill the meat for 1 hour, turning occasionally and brushing with the marinade. Remove the meat from the grill; leave the fire going.

3. Place the meat in the center of a large piece of heavy-duty aluminum foil. Remove the onion slices from the marinade and place on top of the meat along with the carrot slices. Pour about ½ cup of the reserved marinade over the meat. Fold up and seal the foil well. Continue to grill the foil-wrapped meat over medium coals until it is fork-tender, 1 to 1½ hours longer.

4. Let the meat rest in the foil for 15 minutes before removing it to a platter. Carve the roast across the grain into thin slices. Pour pan juices from the wrap over the meat. Serve each portion with some of the onions and carrots.

Herbed Boneless Roast Beef with Horseradish Sauce

This party recipe is wonderful with a whole tenderloin of beef, but when marinated, then grilled and thinly sliced, the more economical eye of round roast is every bit as tasty.

8 Servings

---

3 pounds tenderloin of beef or eye of round, trimmed
½ cup dry red wine
¼ cup red wine vinegar
¼ cup olive oil
1 tablespoon Dijon mustard
¼ cup chopped shallots
2 garlic cloves, chopped

½ teaspoon salt
½ teaspoon freshly ground pepper
¼ cup prepared white horseradish
¼ cup mayonnaise
¼ cup plain yogurt

Mesquite or hickory chips

---

1. If using a tenderloin, tie the slim end underneath to make a more evenly shaped roast. In a shallow dish just large enough to hold the meat, whisk together the wine, vinegar, olive oil, mustard, shallots, garlic, salt, and pepper. Add the meat and turn to coat. Cover and refrigerate at least 6 hours and up to 24 hours, turning occasionally. (The eye of round should be marinated for at least 12 hours.) Return to room temperature before cooking.

2. To make the sauce, stir together the horseradish, mayonnaise, and yogurt. Cover and refrigerate for at least 2 hours and up to 2 days. Remove from the refrigerator 30 minutes before serving.

---

3. Soak the wood chips in cold water for at least 30 minutes. Prepare a medium-hot fire in a covered charcoal or gas grill. Just before cooking, toss the wet chips onto the hot coals or add to a gas grill according to the manufacturer's directions. Remove the meat from the marinade and pat dry with paper towels. Grill, turning 3 or 4 times to cook evenly, until it is well browned on the outside and the internal temperature on an instant-reading thermometer registers 120 degrees for rare meat or 130 degrees for medium-rare, a total of about 25 to 35 minutes.

4. Let the meat rest for about 10 minutes before slicing. Thinly slice the eye of round roast; cut the tenderloin into ½-inch-thick slices. Serve with the horseradish sauce on the side.

Big Ben's Ribs

Though beef ribs can be cooked to falling-off-the bone tenderness directly on the grill, I prefer partially cooking them first in foil (either on the grill or in the oven. Then the ribs can be finished over higher heat to produce the wonderfully tender meat with a crisp, caramelized crust so prized by my big friend, Ben.

4 to 6 Servings

---

1 cup bottled chili sauce
3 tablespoons bourbon
2 tablespoons cider vinegar
2 tablespoons honey
1 tablespoon vegetable oil
1 tablespoon Worcestershire sauce

1 tablespoon prepared white
 horseradish
½ teaspoon freshly ground pepper
4 pounds meaty, well-trimmed beef
 short ribs, cut crosswise into 2-inch
 pieces

---

1. In a shallow dish large enough to hold the ribs, combine the chili sauce, bourbon, vinegar, honey, oil, Worcestershire, horseradish, and pepper. Add the meat and turn to coat all over with the marinade. Cover and refrigerate at least 8 hours or up to 24 hours.

2. Prepare a medium fire in a covered charcoal or gas grill or preheat the oven to 350 degrees. Wrap the meat, coated with its marinade, in a large piece of heavy-duty aluminum foil. Crimp the edges to seal the package well. Grill or bake until the meat is tender, 1 to 1½ hours. (The meat can be cooked several hours ahead. Return to room temperature before finishing the cooking.)

3. Prepare a hot fire in a covered charcoal or gas grill. Remove the ribs from the foil and grill, brushing with the marinade and turning once or twice, until all sides are richly browned, about 8 to 10 minutes.

Korean Beef Ribs

Beef ribs are a real treat when done right, and the Koreans are experts. It is important to buy really good-quality ribs, preferably cut from the tender, "prime" back rib section if you want to cook them the fashionable Korean way to medium-rare. If you use chuck short ribs and want them falling off the bone, follow the cooking method for Big Ben's Ribs on p. 84.

4 to 6 Servings

⅓ cup toasted sesame seeds (see Note below)

¼ cup soy sauce

2 tablespoons rice wine vinegar

1½ tablespoons peanut oil

1 tablespoon Asian sesame oil

1 tablespoon grated fresh ginger

1 tablespoon brown sugar

½ teaspoon crushed hot pepper

2 garlic cloves, minced

½ cup chopped scallions

4 pounds meaty beef ribs, cut into individual rib sections

---

1. In a shallow dish large enough to hold the meat, combine the sesame seeds, soy sauce, vinegar, peanut oil, sesame oil, ginger, brown sugar, hot pepper, garlic, and scallions. Add the meat and turn to coat all over with the marinade. Cover and refrigerate for at least 4 hours and up to 24 hours, turning often.

2. Build a medium-hot fire in a covered charcoal or gas grill. Grill the ribs over the coals, turning and brushing 2 or 3 times with the marinade, until medium-rare, a total of about 15 minutes.

NOTE: To toast sesame seeds, place in a small dry frying pan and stir over medium heat for about 3 minutes, until they darken slightly and become fragrant. Immediately remove from the pan to prevent burning.

Mother's Barbecued Meat Loaves

My mother is a terrific cook and barbecued "meat loaves" are one of her originals. Shaped like a thick, oval patty, the meat loaf mixture grills to a juicy interior with a crispy crust, just like a good meat loaf should be. If your butcher carries a good unseasoned meat loaf mixture, you can use it in place of the three meats listed.

6 Servings

---

1 pound ground chuck
¼ pound ground veal
¼ pound ground pork
⅓ cup finely chopped onion
¼ cup chopped parsley
1 teaspoon dry mustard
1 teaspoon salt
½ teaspoon freshly ground pepper

¼ teaspoon grated nutmeg
½ cup fine fresh bread crumbs
1 egg, lightly beaten
2 tablespoons milk
1 cup barbecue sauce, commercial or homemade All-American Barbecue Sauce (p. 42)

---

1. In a mixing bowl, use your hands to blend lightly but thoroughly the ground meats, onion, parsley, mustard, salt, pepper, nutmeg, bread crumbs, egg, and milk. Gently form the mixture into 6 oval loaves about ¾ inch thick. (The meat loaves can be formed early in the day and refrigerated, covered, until ready to grill.)
2. Prepare a medium-hot fire in a covered charcoal or gas grill. Grill the meat loaves, turning 2 or 3 times with a wide spatula and brushing several times with the barbecue sauce, until no longer pink in the center and well browned and crisp on the outside, about 12 to 15 minutes.

The Best Burger and the Works

Burgers and the backyard barbecue are such a common team that we have come to take them for granted. There is one important requirement for making the best burgers—the meat. Freshly ground chuck is definitely the cut of choice.

6 Servings

---

2 pounds freshly ground (never frozen) chuck (80% to 85% lean)
Salt and freshly ground pepper
6 very fresh hamburger buns, each about 4 inches in diameter
6 slices of perfectly ripe beefsteak tomato

6 thin slices of sweet onion, such as Vidalia or Maui
6 leaves of tender lettuce
Optional additions: Dijon mustard, good ketchup, mayonnaise, thin slices of cheese

---

1. Prepare a medium-hot fire in a covered charcoal or gas grill. Divide the meat into 6 portions and shape into patties about 4 inches in diameter. Handle the meat gently, trying not to compact it too much. Season each patty lightly with salt and generously with pepper. Grill, turning only once, to desired degree of doneness, about 5 to 7 minutes per side for medium-rare, 6 to 8 minutes per side for medium, or longer for well done.

2. A couple of minutes before the burgers are done, place the buns, cut sides down, on the grill and lightly toast them.

3. Assemble the burgers with the meat, then tomato, onion, and lettuce. Add the options as desired. (If you are using cheese, it can be melted on the burger during the last minute of cooking or can be added when making the sandwich.)

Cajun Burgers

The peppery and spicy flavors of "blackened" foods have become so popular that the original fish cooking technique seems to have been extended to nearly everything except doughnuts. But the concept of a blackened, or Cajun, burger is a particularly good one, since the juiciness of the meat tempers and enhances the richness of the spice blend. I like these served on slightly crusty buns or in sourdough rolls, slathered with a thin coating of mayonnaise enlivened with a little lemon juice.

6 Servings

1 tablespoon paprika	2 pounds ground chuck
1 tablespoon chili powder	¼ cup mayonnaise
1 teaspoon onion powder	2 teaspoons lemon juice
1 teaspoon garlic powder	6 good-quality slightly crusty ham-
¾ teaspoon salt	burger buns or sourdough sandwich
½ teaspoon black pepper	rolls
½ teaspoon ground white pepper	6 slices of meaty tomato, each about
½ teaspoon cayenne	¼ inch thick
½ teaspoon ground cumin	

1. Prepare a medium-hot fire in a covered charcoal or gas grill. In a small dish, combine the paprika, chili powder, onion powder, garlic powder, salt, black pepper, white pepper, cayenne, and cumin. Divide the meat into 6 portions and gently form each into a patty about 4 inches in diameter. Liberally sprinkle both sides of the patties with some of the seasoning mixture, coating evenly. In a small dish, stir together the mayonnaise and lemon juice.

2. Grill the burgers, turning once, about 5 to 7 minutes for medium-rare, about 6 to 8 minutes per side for medium. A couple of minutes before the burgers are done, place the buns, cut sides down, on the grill and lightly toast them.

3. Assemble the burgers by spreading the flavored mayonnaise on the cut sides of the buns, then adding the grilled meat patties and tomato slices.

Bruschetta Burgers

This is my favorite dressed-up version of a hamburger, probably because it combines the ripe tomatoes and fresh basil that seem to be the very culinary essence of summer.

6 Servings

¼ cup olive oil
1 tablespoon balsamic vinegar
1 large garlic clove, minced
¼ teaspoon crushed hot pepper
2 pounds ground chuck
Salt and freshly ground pepper
6 thin slices of mozzarella cheese
　(about 3 ounces)

12 slices of Italian bread, cut between
　¼ and ½ inch thick
6 thin slices of sweet onion
6 slices of ripe, meaty tomato
12 large fresh basil leaves

---

1. Prepare a medium-hot fire in a covered charcoal or gas grill. In a small bowl, whisk together the olive oil, vinegar, garlic, and pepper flakes. Let stand about 15 minutes. Divide the meat into 6 portions and gently form each into a patty about 4 inches in diameter. Season both sides lightly with salt and pepper.

2. Grill the meat, turning once, to desired degree of doneness, about 5 to 7 minutes per side for medium-rare, 6 to 8 minutes per side for medium. About 2 minutes before the burgers are done, set a slice of mozzarella on top of each burger. Grill the bread about 45 seconds per side, until lightly toasted. Brush one side of the toasted bread with the olive oil mixture.

3. Assemble the burgers by placing the patties on 6 of the toast slices, brushed sides up. Add the onion, tomato, and basil leaves, then top with the remaining toast slices, brushed sides down.

　　　　　　　　Beef, Veal, and Venison

Grilled Liver and Onions

This is a recipe for liver haters. The grill does magical things for the taste of liver, especially when it is smothered in grilled onions.

4 Servings

1 pound calf's liver, cut between ¼
   and ½ inch thick
½ teaspoon salt
¼ teaspoon freshly ground pepper
1½ teaspoons dried thyme leaves

¾ teaspoon dried marjoram
1 large sweet onion, such as Vidalia or
   Maui
2 tablespoons olive oil

1. Prepare a hot fire in a covered charcoal or gas grill.

2. Season the liver on both sides with the salt, pepper, 1 teaspoon of the thyme, and ½ teaspoon of the marjoram. Cut the onion crosswise into ¼-inch-thick slices. Combine the olive oil with the remaining ½ teaspoon thyme and ¼ teaspoon marjoram. Brush the onion slices with the oil.

3. Grill the liver in the center of the grill and the onions to the sides, turning once with a wide spatula, until the liver is just pink in the center and the onions are browned and tender, a total of 5 to 6 minutes. Serve the liver topped with the grilled onion slices.

Grilled Veal Chops with Triple Tomato Compote

The compote that accompanies veal here is delicious on just about anything, even by the spoonful all by itself along with a hunk of good bread. The sauce combines sun-dried tomatoes with fresh red and yellow tomatoes, which are becoming increasingly available in summer markets. If you can't find them, just use more fresh red tomatoes.

4 Servings

½ cup dry white wine
1 large garlic clove, minced
¼ cup sun-dried tomatoes (about 1 ounce)
½ pound red tomatoes, seeded and coarsely chopped
½ pound yellow tomatoes, seeded and coarsely chopped

⅓ cup thinly sliced scallions
¼ cup chopped fresh basil
½ teaspoon salt
¼ teaspoon freshly ground pepper
¼ cup extra-virgin olive oil
4 center-cut veal chops, cut about 1 inch thick (each about 8 ounces)

1. In a small nonaluminum saucepan, bring the wine, garlic, and sun-dried tomatoes to a simmer. Remove from the heat and let stand for 20 minutes to plump the tomatoes. Drain the wine from the saucepan into a mixing bowl. Coarsely chop the tomatoes and add them to the bowl, along with the chopped red and yellow tomatoes, scallions, basil, salt, pepper, and 3 tablespoons of the olive oil. Let the tomato compote stand at room temperature about 15 minutes or refrigerate up to 4 hours before using, but return to room temperature to serve.

2. Prepare a hot fire in a covered charcoal or gas grill. Brush both sides of the veal chops with the remaining olive oil. Season with additional salt and pepper. Grill the veal, turning once or twice, until just cooked through and no longer pink, a total of about 15 to 18 minutes.

3. Serve the chops topped with a spoonful of the tomato compote.

Grilled Tarragon-Mustard Veal Cutlets

This is so quick and easy, but makes a fabulous main course for entertaining, especially when accompanied by Grilled Ratatouille (p. 182). The tarragon and mustard mixture is also delicious on pork cutlets.

6 Servings

⅓ cup Dijon mustard
2 tablespoons chopped fresh tarragon
  or 2 teaspoons dried
1½ pounds veal cutlets from the leg

or shoulder, each between ¼ and
  ½ inch thick
Freshly ground pepper

1. Prepare a hot fire in a covered charcoal or gas grill.
2. In a small dish, combine the mustard and tarragon. Season both sides of the veal with pepper, then smear with the mustard mixture. Let stand 15 to 30 minutes.
3. Grill the meat, turning once, until browned and just cooked through, about 2 to 3 minutes per side.

Swedish Vealburgers

With the same flavors that characterize Swedish meatballs, these vealburgers are sauced with plain yogurt instead of high-fat sour cream.

4 Servings

1 pound ground veal	½ teaspoon salt
1 cup fresh white bread crumbs	¼ teaspoon freshly ground pepper
½ cup finely chopped onion	1 egg, lightly beaten
¼ cup chopped fresh dill, plus sprigs	1 cup plain yogurt
for garnish	½ teaspoon ground nutmeg

1. Prepare a hot fire in a covered charcoal or gas grill. Use your hands to blend the veal, bread crumbs, onion, dill, salt, pepper, and egg in a mixing bowl. Form into 4 patties, each about ¾ inch thick. In a smaller bowl, combine the yogurt and nutmeg.

2. Grill the veal patties, turning once, until barely pink to the center, about 6 to 7 minutes per side. Serve the patties with a dollop of the flavored yogurt on top. Garnish with dill sprigs.

Grilled Venison Steaks with Peppered Apples

6 Servings

¾ cup dry red wine
¼ cup gin
3 tablespoons olive oil
1 tablespoon crushed juniper berries
2 strips of lemon peel, each about 1 inch long
2 strips of orange peel, each about 1 inch long

½ teaspoon salt
1 teaspoon coarsely ground pepper
6 venison steaks, cut ¾ to 1 inch thick (4 to 5 ounces each)
2 tablespoons apple jelly
1 large tart apple, cored, peeled, and cut crosswise into 6 rings, each about ¼ inch thick

1. In a shallow dish just large enough to hold the meat, combine the wine, gin, olive oil, juniper berries, lemon peel, orange peel, salt, and ½ teaspoon of the pepper. Remove and reserve ¼ cup of the liquid marinade, then add the meat to the dish and turn to coat both sides. Cover and refrigerate at least 8 hours or up to 24 hours. Return to room temperature before cooking.

2. Prepare a hot fire in a covered charcoal or gas grill. Remove the steaks from the marinade and grill, turning once and basting occasionally with the marinade, until they reach a desired degree of doneness, 10 to 13 minutes for medium-rare.

3. While the venison steaks are grilling, combine the ¼ cup reserved marinade with the remaining ½ teaspoon pepper and the apple jelly in a small nonaluminum saucepan. Cook over medium-low heat, stirring, just until the jelly melts.

4. About 5 minutes before the meat is done, brush both sides of the apple slices with the jelly sauce and grill, turning once or twice and brushing again with the jelly, until just tender and tinged with brown.

Chapter Four
Pork, Ham, Sausage, and Ribs

To many purists, barbecue means pork, whether it is a falling-apart pork shoulder or crusty ribs. In fact, folks are so devoted to pork barbecue that it is difficult to agree on what constitutes the quintessential all-American pork barbecue. Natives from three of the most staunchly proud pork barbecue regions of the country—North Carolina, Memphis, and Kansas City—all insist that theirs is the authentic version. Truth is, any good pork barbecue is well worth eating!

Pork today is leaner than ever before, so cooking times are shorter and marinades and sauces more important to impart juiciness and flavor. Older recipes are likely to yield tough results; it is worth trying the new, shorter cooking methods. Be sure to cook pork until no longer pink (large cuts can be tested with an instant-reading thermometer to 160 degrees), but take care not to overcook, or it will dry out. Let roasts stand about 10 minutes before carving.

Pork chops are the most common cut for home barbecues, and they are still a favorite. But be sure to try the newly popular—and much leaner—pork tenderloins, which are like miniroasts, or boneless pork chops, and can be as tender as a good steak. Both cook in mere minutes. Pork shoulder steaks need longer cooking, but their flavor is incomparable. Similarly, pork butt or shoulder roasts are the stuff from which real "barbecue" is made. These cuts are usually flavored with either a marinade or a spice rub, followed by a long, slow cooking for best results. Home smokers are ideal for this (see Smoking, page 196), but a covered grill with an indirect fire also works well.

Lemon and Fennel Grilled Pork Tenderloin

The delicate licorice taste of fennel is deepened and enriched by grilling. This easy main course is elegant enough for any guest, especially when accompanied by a parsleyed rice pilaf and sugar snap peas. If you don't have any Pernod, the anise-flavored liqueur, use 1 tablespoon lemon juice instead.

6 Servings

1½ teaspoons fennel seeds
2 garlic cloves, crushed through a
  press
1½ teaspoons grated lemon zest
½ teaspoon salt

½ teaspoon freshly ground pepper
2 tablespoons olive oil
1 tablespoon Pernod
2 pork tenderloins, trimmed of excess
  fat (about 2 pounds total)

1. Using a mortar and pestle or a flat mallet or in a spice grinder, crush the fennel seeds. In a small bowl, stir together the crushed fennel, garlic, lemon zest, salt, pepper, olive oil, and Pernod. Smear the mixture evenly over the tenderloins.
2. Prepare a medium-hot fire in a covered charcoal or gas grill. Oil the grill rack. Grill the pork, turning occasionally, until the meat is no longer pink in the center and the internal temperature on an instant-reading thermometer registers 160 degrees, about 15 to 20 minutes.
3. Let the meat rest 5 minutes before cutting into thin slices.

Grilled Apple- and Sage-Stuffed Pork Roast

A boneless pork loin is called for here, which is butterflied in step 3. If you have your butcher prepare the meat, say you want it boned and butterflied. There are all sorts of good things to stuff in a pork roast, but few are better than apples. I particularly like this recipe for a late summer supper when the evenings are likely to turn a little cool. Applewood chips and fresh sage leaves on the fire enhance the flavor of the stuffing.

6 Servings

---

1 cup apple cider or water
½ cup dried apple chunks (about 2 ounces)
2 tablespoons olive oil
½ cup thinly sliced onion
2 tablespoons chopped fresh sage or 2 teaspoons dried

Salt and freshly ground pepper
1 boneless pork loin (about 2½ pounds)

4 or 5 handfuls applewood chips, optional
6 or 8 sprigs fresh sage, optional

---

1. Heat the cider or water just to boiling, then pour it over the dried apples in a small bowl. Let stand until cool and the liquid is absorbed, about 20 minutes.
2. In a medium frying pan, heat the olive oil. Add the onion and cook over medium heat, stirring often, until soft, 3 to 5 minutes. Add half of the chopped sage and season lightly with salt and pepper. Stir to blend. Let cool, then use a slotted spoon to remove the onions and add to the apples. Reserve the oil in the pan.
3. Butterfly the pork roast by cutting down the length of the meat halfway through; then open it up like a book. Spread the onion and apples over the cut side of the meat. Fold the roast back to its original shape and tie securely with wet kitchen

string. Rub the outside of the roast with the reserved oil in the frying pan. Season lightly with salt and pepper.

4. If using wood chips, soak them in cold water for at least 30 minutes. Prepare a medium fire in a covered charcoal or gas grill. Just before cooking, toss half of the chips onto the coals; add the remainder halfway through the cooking time, or add to a gas grill according to the manufacturer's instructions. Cook the pork, turning occasionally, until the outside is well browned and the inside temperature registers 160 to 170 degrees on an instant-reading thermometer, about 1¼ hours. If using sage sprigs, add them to the coals about 10 minutes before the meat is done. Let the meat rest about 15 minutes before carving.

Grill-Smoked Pork Chops

These quickly cooked chops taste long-smoked. Serve them with a juicy accompaniment, such as fresh applesauce, or as part of a smoked meat and sauerkraut platter. This treatment works well for ribs, too.

8 Servings

---

3 tablespoons brown sugar

3 tablespoons paprika

1 tablespoon coarsely ground black
   pepper

1 teaspoon salt

8 center-cut pork chops, cut ¾ inch
   thick (about 3 pounds total)

2 or 3 handfuls hickory chips

---

1. In a small dish, stir together the brown sugar, paprika, pepper, and salt. Generously pat the mixture onto both sides of the pork chops. Let the chops stand at room temperature for 30 minutes.

2. Soak the hickory chips in cold water for at least 30 minutes. Prepare a medium-hot fire in a covered charcoal or gas grill. Just before cooking, toss the wet chips onto the coals.

3. Grill the chops, turning once, until nicely browned outside and white to the center, 15 to 20 minutes.

Pork Loin, Red Onion, and Brandied Fig Kebabs

Pork loin is the best cut for kebabs, since it is already tender, which is important since the cooking time is relatively short.

4 Servings

⅓ cup orange juice
¼ cup brandy
2 tablespoons lemon juice
2 tablespoons olive oil
½ teaspoon ground cardamom
½ teaspoon salt
¼ teaspoon freshly ground pepper

1 lemon, thinly sliced
1 pound boneless pork loin, cut in
   1¼-inch chunks
12 whole fresh figs or soft dried figs
1 large red onion, cut into 1-inch
   chunks

1. In a shallow dish just large enough to hold the meat and figs, combine the orange juice, brandy, lemon juice, olive oil, cardamom, salt, pepper, and 8 of the lemon slices. Add the meat and turn to coat. Cover and refrigerate at least 1 hour or up to 8 hours. Add the figs and onions during the last 1 hour of marinating time.
2. Prepare a medium-hot fire in a covered charcoal or gas grill. Thread the meat, onions, figs, and marinated lemon slices, with fruit at the ends, onto metal skewers. Grill, turning occasionally, until the meat is nicely browned and cooked through and the figs are lightly browned, about 10 to 12 minutes. Garnish with the remaining lemon slices.

East St. Louis Barbecued Pork Steaks

I learned how to do this while living in St. Louis, where pork is especially popular. Be sure to use pork steaks cut from the shoulder; the more expensive loin or rib chops simply will not cook up to the correct falling-off-the-bone finish. While these take some time to tenderize, they absorb the wonderful flavor of the barbecue sauce while they are cooking, and the dish is even better prepared a day in advance and reheated. This meat is customarily served with creamy coleslaw and lots of crusty bread to sop up the sauce.

8 to 10 Servings

---

5 to 6 handfuls hickory chips

16 pork shoulder steaks, cut slightly
   less than ½ inch thick (5 to 6
   pounds)

3 quarts water
¼ cup cider vinegar
½ teaspoon crushed hot red pepper
Doctored-Up Barbecue Sauce (recipe
   follows)

---

1. Soak the hickory chips in cold water for at least 30 minutes. Prepare a medium fire in a covered charcoal or gas grill. Just before cooking, toss about half of the wet chips onto the coals, adding the remainder as needed during the cooking process, or add to a gas grill according to the manufacturer's instructions.

2. Trim any excess fat from the pork steaks. In a large saucepan, bring the water, vinegar, and hot pepper to a simmer on a stovetop over high heat. Set the pot at the edge of the grill to keep warm. Place the barbecue sauce in a large nonreactive saucepan or flameproof casserole.

3. You will be cooking the pork steaks in 2 batches. Using long tongs, dip 8 of the pork steaks into the vinegar water and set on the grill. Cook 5 minutes. Dip in vinegar water again, and set back on the grill, turning the pork steaks over. Cook another 5 minutes, then repeat the process 3 more times for a total of 25 minutes' cooking time. When the first batch of pork is done, place the steaks in the barbecue sauce, cover, and heat on the stove so that the steaks simmer slowly in the sauce.

4. Repeat the cooking process with the remaining pork, adding those steaks to the simmering sauce. Simmer the ribs in the sauce, covered, 1½ to 2½ hours, until the meat starts to fall off the bones. (The pork steaks can be completed a day ahead and reheated in the sauce.)

Doctored-Up Barbecue Sauce

I developed this recipe to approximate the local St. Louis brand of barbecue sauce traditionally used with barbecued pork steaks, but have found that it is, in a pinch, a darned good substitute for homemade barbecue sauces. Be sure to sample several brands of commercial sauces first, since this recipe is only as good as the bottled base that goes into it.

Makes about 10 cups

2 tablespoons vegetable oil	4 cups onion-flavored barbecue sauce
1 large onion, chopped	¾ cup chili sauce
2 garlic cloves, crushed through a press	12 ounces beer
4 cups hickory smoke-flavored barbecue sauce	

1. In a large saucepan, heat the oil and cook the onion over medium heat, stirring often, until softened, about 3 minutes. Add the garlic and cook 1 minute. Add all of the remaining ingredients and simmer for 10 minutes, stirring often.

2. Use the sauce immediately or store, covered, in the refrigerator, for up to 1 week.

Polynesian Pork Kebabs with Pineapple and Bananas

The marinade used here is also good with chicken, and I've enjoyed it with swordfish, too. Serve these kebabs with rice tossed with some toasted unsweetened coconut and a spinach salad for an easy supper with an island theme.

6 Servings

1½ cups unsweetened pineapple juice
3 tablespoons soy sauce
2 tablespoons lemon juice
2 tablespoons dry sherry
1 tablespoon honey
½ teaspoon salt
½ teaspoon freshly ground pepper

1½ pounds boneless pork loin, cut into 1-inch chunks
1 small pineapple, cut into 1-inch chunks
2 firm bananas, cut into 1-inch chunks

---

1. Bring the pineapple juice to a boil in a small nonaluminum saucepan. Reduce the heat to medium-low and simmer until reduced by about one-fourth, about 5 minutes. Remove the pan from the heat and stir in the soy sauce, lemon juice, sherry, honey, salt, and pepper. Pour into a small shallow dish and cool to room temperature. Add the pork and stir to coat all sides. Cover and refrigerate at least 2 hours or up to 24 hours. Return to room temperature before cooking.

2. Prepare a hot fire in a covered charcoal or gas grill. Thread the pork and fruits separately onto metal skewers. Brush the pork kebabs with the marinade and grill, turning once or twice and brushing with more marinade, until nicely browned outside and white to the center, about 10 minutes. At the same time, grill the fruits, brushing once with marinade, until tinged with brown, about 5 minutes.

3. To serve, remove meat and fruits from skewers and arrange on a platter.

Ginger-Peachy Barbecued Ham Steaks

This is also a lovely main course for a summer brunch as well as an easy supper, particularly at the height of peach season. Add some home-fried potatoes or quick Grilled Hash Browns (p. 179) and steamed green beans to round out the meal.

6 Servings

½ cup peach preserves
½ cup lemon juice
1 teaspoon ground ginger
1 teaspoon dry mustard
½ teaspoon freshly ground pepper

1½ pounds ham steak, cut ½ to ¾ inch thick
3 ripe but firm peaches, halved and pitted

---

1. Prepare a hot fire in a covered charcoal or gas grill. In a small saucepan, heat the preserves, lemon juice, ginger, mustard, and pepper over medium-low heat, stirring until the preserves melt and the sauce is smooth, 2 to 3 minutes. Brush both sides of the ham and all of the peaches with the sauce.

2. Grill the ham, turning once and brushing with more sauce, until golden brown, about 10 minutes total. At the same time, grill the peaches at the side or cooler part of the grill, turning once, until tinged with brown, about 5 minutes total.

Grill-Smoked Ham

Here is a good way to dress up an ordinary supermarket cooked ham shank or butt half. The smoky flavor comes from the wood chips and wet corncobs tossed directly onto the coals. Dried corncobs are available at specialty stores or from mail-order sources that sell specialty wood chips, or even from farm feed stores.

8 Servings

---

1 fully cooked ham shank or butt half (4 to 4½ pounds)
8 to 10 whole cloves
¼ cup orange juice
¼ cup maple syrup
2 tablespoons Dijon mustard

½ teaspoon freshly ground pepper

5 to 6 handfuls maple or hickory wood chips
2 dried corncobs, optional

---

1. Trim most of the excess fat from the ham, but leave a ¼-inch layer. Score the fatty top in a diamond shape; stud the diamonds with the cloves. In a small bowl, blend together the orange juice, maple syrup, mustard, and pepper. Brush all over the ham. Let the ham stand 30 minutes at room temperature.

2. Soak the wood chips and corncobs in cold water for at least 30 minutes. If using a covered charcoal grill, prepare a medium fire. When the coals are ready, carefully lift the grate and push them to one side of the grill. Set a disposable foil pan opposite the coals and pour about ½ inch of water into the pan. Toss half of the wet chips onto the coals and set the corncobs in the water pan. Add the remaining chips to the coals about halfway through the cooking time. Or prepare an indirect fire in a gas grill and add the wood chips according to the manufacturer's directions. The corncobs will have to be cut up to fit into the wood receptacle as well.

3. Place the ham on the grill over the water pan. Cook without turning, until the ham is browned and the internal temperature on a meat thermometer registers 140 degrees, about 1 hour. Let stand for about 15 minutes before slicing thin.

Southwest Pork Burgers

If you have access to chorizo sausage meat or another peppery pork sausage meat, substitute it for half of the ground pork. If you are in a real hurry, you can season the ground pork with packaged taco seasoning mix, but I like the ability to control the quality of the herbs and spices and level of salt by adding my own.

6 Servings

---

1 egg
1½ pounds lean ground pork
¼ cup unseasoned dry bread crumbs
2 tablespoons milk
1 tablespoon chili powder
½ teaspoon ground cumin
½ teaspoon dried oregano

½ teaspoon salt
⅛ teaspoon cayenne
6 thin slices of Monterey Jack cheese
6 sandwich rolls, preferably cornmeal
   rolls
1 cup bottled salsa or taco sauce
1½ cups shredded iceberg lettuce

---

1. Prepare a medium-hot fire in a covered charcoal or gas grill.
2. In a mixing bowl, beat the egg, then add the meat, bread crumbs, milk, chili powder, cumin, oregano, salt, and cayenne. Use your hands to mix the ingredients thoroughly. Form into 6 patties about ½ inch thick.
3. Grill the patties, turning once, until well browned on the outside and no longer pink in the center, about 15 to 17 minutes. Top each patty with a slice of cheese and place the rolls, cut sides down, on the grill. Cook about 30 seconds to melt the cheese and lightly toast the rolls.
4. Garnish the burgers with the salsa and shredded lettuce.

Grilled Italian Sausage Burgers

4 Servings

1¼ pounds fennel-seasoned Italian sausage meat, sweet or hot
1 medium-sized fennel bulb with leaves
2 tablespoons olive oil
1 garlic clove, crushed through a press

4 thick slices of beefsteak tomato
Salt and freshly ground pepper
8 slices of seeded Italian bread, cut about ½ inch thick
1 small bunch of arugula or 4 romaine lettuce leaves

---

1. Form the sausage into 4 patties about 3 inches in diameter. Cut off the fennel stalks and reserve the feathery green leaves. Trim and quarter the fennel bulb. In a small dish, combine the olive oil and garlic.

2. Prepare a medium-hot fire in a covered charcoal or gas grill. Just before cooking, dampen the fennel leaves under water and toss them onto the coals. Brush the fennel bulb quarters lightly with some of the garlic oil. Set them at the side of the grill where the heat is less intense. Place the sausage patties in the center of the grill. Cook, turning the patties and the fennel once or twice, until the fennel bulbs are tender and browned and the sausage patties are no longer pink in the center, about 12 to 16 minutes.

3. A couple of minutes before the fennel and sausage are done, brush both sides of the tomato slices with some garlic oil and grill, turning once, until grill marks just begin to appear, about 1 minute per side. Remove the meat and vegetables to a plate. Slice the fennel. Brush one side of the bread slices with any remaining garlic oil and grill until lightly toasted on both sides, about 30 seconds per side.

4. Construct the burgers with the oiled sides of the bread sandwiching the sausage, fennel slices, tomatoes, and arugula.

The Ultimate Hot Dog

Hot dogs have taken a lot of heat lately, sometimes for just cause. There are all sorts of hot dogs on the market, from very good to awful, and in this case, you usually get what you pay for. Generally, the best hot dogs are those that are sold by the pound at the meat counter, in a casing like other sausages. There are excellent turkey frankfurters on the market, and also beef franks, but the classic hot dog is still made of pork, though the others can be cooked in the same way. For the best appearance, the bun should be about ½ inch shorter than the frankfurter, so that the ends can stick out slightly in the traditional way. Condiments are to taste, but connoisseurs frown on ketchup.

6 Servings

---

6 frankfurters in casings (1 to 1¼ pounds), lightly scored
6 high-quality frankfurter buns

1 tablespoon butter, melted
Mustard, pickle relish, sauerkraut, chili sauce

---

1. Prepare a hot fire in a covered charcoal or gas grill. Grill the frankfurters, turning carefully with tongs to heat completely and produce grill marks on all sides, about 5 to 8 minutes. Skins should just begin to split when frankfurters are done.

2. A couple of minutes before the frankfurters are done, brush the cut sides of the buns with the melted butter, then grill the cut sides just until lightly toasted, about 2 minutes.

3. Place the frankfurters in the buns and garnish with desired condiments.

Grilled Brats and Circus Onions

My fondest childhood memory of the circus coming to town is not of acrobats or elephants, but of the grilled bratwurst smothered in greasy-good onions and peppers sold from carts on the midway. To this day, the combination is called "circus onions" at our house, but my modern recipe is a little more adult, with less grease and a splash of beer to flavor the onions.

6 Servings

---

1 large onion, thinly sliced
1 large green bell pepper, thinly sliced
2 tablespoons vegetable oil
2 garlic cloves, crushed through a
    press
¾ teaspoon caraway seeds
½ cup beer

¼ teaspoon salt
⅛ teaspoon freshly ground pepper
6 bratwurst or knockwurst (about 1
    pound total)
6 frankfurter buns
Grainy mustard

---

1. Prepare a hot fire in a covered charcoal or gas grill.

2. In a large frying pan, cook the onion and pepper in the oil over medium heat until the vegetables are softened, about 3 minutes. Add the garlic and caraway seeds and cook until the onions are golden, about 2 minutes. Add the beer and cook until the liquid is reduced by about half, about 3 minutes. Season with the salt and pepper. Remove from the heat and cover to keep warm.

3. Split the bratwurst lengthwise, but do not cut all the way through. Grill until nicely browned on both sides, about 8 minutes. During the last 2 minutes of cooking, set the buns, cut sides down, at the edge of the grill to toast lightly.

4. To serve, spread the cut sides of the buns with mustard, add a bratwurst, then spoon on the pepper and onion mixture.

Grilled Italian Sausage and Pepper Hero

Whether you call it a sub, a grinder, or a hero, this is a great sandwich made with either hot or sweet sausage. Because the sausage is precooked indoors, it is also a quick fix on the grill.

4 Servings

---

1 pound Italian sausage links, sweet or hot
¾ cup dry red or white wine
2 tablespoons olive oil

1 garlic clove, crushed through a press
2 green bell peppers, quartered
2 red bell peppers, quartered
4 long hero or sandwich rolls, split

---

1. Prick the sausages in several places. In a medium frying pan, cook the sausages in the wine over medium heat, turning frequently, until the liquid is nearly evaporated, about 8 minutes. (The sausages can be precooked several hours ahead and refrigerated. Return to room temperature before grilling.)

2. Prepare a medium-hot fire in a covered charcoal or gas grill. In a small dish, combine the olive oil and garlic. Let stand 15 minutes, then brush all sides of the peppers with some of the garlic oil. Cut the sausages almost in half lengthwise so that they will lie flat on the grill.

3. Grill the peppers, turning often, until they have softened and the skins are well browned, about 10 minutes. Place the peppers in a bag and let them steam for 5 minutes, then peel off and discard the skins. Cut the peppers into ½-inch strips.

4. Meanwhile, grill the sausages until browned on all sides, 5 to 7 minutes. Brush the cut sides of the rolls with more of the garlic oil and grill, cut sides down, on the side of the grill until lightly toasted, about 1 minute.

5. Assemble the sandwiches with the sausages and peppers, brushing the peppers with any remaining garlic oil.

Grilled Deviled Pork Cutlets

Pork cutlets are increasingly popular since they are quite lean, cook quickly, and are exceptionally versatile, much like boneless chicken breasts. This is a particularly tasty way to grill them; the coating seals in the flavor and adds a dimension not always obtained with quick grilling.

4 Servings

¼ cup grainy Dijon mustard
3 tablespoons orange juice
1 tablespoon Worcestershire sauce

¼ teaspoon freshly ground pepper
1 pound boneless pork cutlets, cut
  about ⅜ inch thick

---

1. In a small dish, whisk together the mustard, orange juice, Worcestershire sauce, and pepper until blended. Smear the coating over both sides of the pork and let the cutlets stand at room temperature for about 30 minutes.
2. Prepare a hot fire in a covered charcoal or gas grill. Grill the pork, turning once, until cooked through, about 8 minutes total.

Real Good Ribs

This is the easiest and most foolproof way to cook ribs, and the homemade sauce is quick and simple. The precooking can even be done a day ahead.

6 Servings

1 small onion, chopped
1 large garlic clove, crushed through a press
2 tablespoons vegetable oil
1 cup chili sauce
⅓ cup molasses

¼ cup Worcestershire sauce
2 tablespoons cider vinegar
½ teaspoon freshly ground pepper
6 pounds pork spareribs
Salt

1. In a medium nonaluminum saucepan, cook the onion and garlic in the oil over medium heat until softened, about 3 minutes. Add the chili sauce, molasses, Worcestershire sauce, vinegar, and pepper. Bring to a boil, reduce the heat to medium-low, and simmer, stirring often, until thickened slightly, about 10 minutes. (The sauce can be made a week ahead and refrigerated. Reheat before using.)

2. Prepare a medium-hot fire in a charcoal or gas grill, or preheat the oven to 350 degrees. If cooking on a grill, wrap the ribs in heavy-duty aluminum foil and grill, turning occasionally, until nearly tender, about 1 hour. If cooking in the oven, place the ribs in a roasting pan and roast for 45 minutes to 1 hour, until nearly tender.

3. Drain off all fat from cooking, then brush the ribs with some of the sauce. Cook directly on the grill, turning often and brushing with more sauce, until well browned and crisp on the outside, about 30 minutes. Cut into sections to serve.

Memphis Dry Ribs

In Memphis, considered by some to be the rib capital of the world, the ribs are barbecued with a dry seasoning coating, then served with a spicy tomato-based sauce on the side. The exact seasonings are hotly debated among residents and closely guarded by cooks. Here, after many samplings, is my admittedly Yankee-based interpretation.

6 Servings

---

1 tablespoon salt	6 pounds pork spareribs
2 teaspoons coarsely ground black pepper	Memphis Rib Sauce (recipe follows)
½ teaspoon crushed hot red pepper	4 to 6 handfuls hickory chips

---

1. Combine the salt, black pepper, and hot pepper in a small bowl. Rub the mixture well all over the ribs. Let the ribs stand at room temperature for 1 hour or refrigerate for 4 hours or up to 24 hours. Return to room temperature before cooking.

2. Soak the hickory chips in cold water for at least 30 minutes. Prepare a medium-hot fire in a covered charcoal grill. Push the coals to the side. Or prepare an indirect fire in a gas grill according to the manufacturer's directions. Just before cooking, toss about half of the wood chips onto the hot coals or add to a gas grill according to the manufacturer's directions.

3. Grill the ribs on the side away from the coals, turning 2 or 3 times, until tender and crusty on the outside, about 1½ hours. Add the remaining wet chips to the coals about halfway through the cooking time. Serve the ribs with the sauce on the side.

Memphis Rib Sauce

In Memphis, a sauce of this type is often served as an accompaniment and a dip for dry barbecued ribs. It also makes a fine barbecue sauce for chicken or pork chops.

Makes about 3 cups

2 cups bottled chili sauce
⅓ cup ketchup
⅓ cup cider vinegar
⅓ cup dark brown sugar
3 tablespoons soy sauce
3 tablespoons dry sherry

1½ teaspoons ground ginger
¾ to 1 teaspoon crushed hot red pepper, to taste
2 garlic cloves, crushed through a press

1. In a medium nonaluminum saucepan, combine all of the ingredients. Simmer over medium-low heat, stirring occasionally, until the sauce just coats a spoon, about 20 minutes. If the sauce thickens too much, thin with a little water.

2. Use immediately or cover and refrigerate for up to 1 week.

Lake Logan Ribs

This is the way they cook ribs at my favorite barbecue place in North Carolina. The "moppin' sauce" is also the dipping sauce. To avoid contamination, just be sure to bring it to a full boil before using it as a dipping sauce.

6 Servings

---

6 pounds pork spareribs
2 teaspoons salt
2 teaspoons freshly ground pepper
¾ cup cider vinegar
2 tablespoons vegetable oil
2 tablespoons brown sugar

1½ tablespoons Worcestershire sauce
1½ teaspoons dry mustard
½ teaspoon cayenne
½ teaspoon Tabasco or other hot pepper sauce, or more to taste

4 or 5 handfuls hickory chips

---

1. Season both sides of the ribs with the salt and pepper. Let stand 15 minutes. In a small nonaluminum saucepan, bring the vinegar, oil, brown sugar, Worcestershire, mustard, and cayenne to a simmer. Remove from the heat and set aside, covered.

2. Soak the hickory chips in cold water for at least 30 minutes. Prepare a medium fire in a covered charcoal or gas grill. Just before cooking, toss about half of the chips onto the hot coals; add remaining chips to the fire about halfway through the cooking time. Or add chips to a gas grill according to the manufacturer's directions. Brush both sides of the ribs with some of the warm sauce, then grill, turning and brushing with sauce several times more, until cooked through and crispy outside, about 1 hour.

3. Bring the remaining sauce to a full boil, cook 2 minutes, then remove from the heat and add the Tabasco. Serve with the ribs for dipping.

Molasses-Rum Country-Style Ribs

Country-style ribs aren't really ribs in the pure sense; they are cut from the shoulder end of the loin and are meatier, more like pork chops. Precooking in the oven, which can be done ahead, leaves half an hour or less on the grill.

6 Servings

---

6 pounds country-style pork ribs
Salt and freshly ground pepper
⅓ cup molasses

⅓ cup dark rum
⅓ cup cider vinegar
3 tablespoons Dijon mustard

---

1. Preheat the oven to 350 degrees. Season the ribs lightly with salt and generously with pepper. Place on a rack in a baking pan, cover tightly with aluminum foil, and bake 30 minutes.

2. Prepare a medium-hot fire in a covered charcoal or gas grill. In a small dish, whisk together the molasses, rum, cider vinegar, and mustard until well blended. Generously brush some of the sauce over both sides of the meat.

3. Grill, turning occasionally and brushing with more sauce, until the outside is crisp and the meat is tender, about 20 to 30 minutes.

Chapter Five

Lamb

There is little better to feast on than a boneless leg of lamb done to a juicy turn on a grill, but lamb kebabs run a close second for favorite party food. Lamb's naturally assertive taste takes beautifully to the smokiness of covered grilling and all manner of exotic marinades, sauces, and/or the addition of aromatic woods or herbs to the fire. Barbecued lamb has long been classic in Greece, in parts of India, and in the Middle East, where the meat is enhanced by fragrant spices, fruits, and vegetables.

If you buy good-quality young lamb, it will have a natural tenderness and distinctive, yet not overpowering flavor. Though it is traditionally called "spring" lamb for the natural season, new methods of breeding yield excellent lamb almost all year long—certainly throughout the barbecue season.

For easiest cooking and best results, trim all excess fat from the lamb, leaving only a thin coating. Use hearty marinades and follow the same directions as for beef. The thinner cuts can stand for a couple of hours at room temperature and larger pieces should be refrigerated, turning in the marinade for up to 2 days to allow as much flavor as possible to permeate the meat.

Cook lamb to the desired degree of doneness, but remember to remove roasts and large pieces from the grill a few minutes earlier to allow for continued cooking while you let the meat rest before carving.

Hunan Barbecued Lamb

This is an easy version of a hot and spicy Hunan-style barbecue. The marinade also works well for beef flank steak.

6 Servings

---

3 pounds boned and butterflied leg of
    lamb
½ cup hoisin sauce
3 tablespoons soy sauce
3 tablespoons dry sherry
2 tablespoons Asian sesame oil

2 tablespoons honey
1 tablespoon grated orange zest
2 teaspoons hot chili oil
2 garlic cloves, crushed through a
    press

---

1. Trim all excess fat from the lamb. In a shallow dish just large enough to hold the lamb, combine the hoisin sauce, soy sauce, sherry, sesame oil, honey, orange zest, chili oil, and garlic. Add the lamb and turn to coat completely. Refrigerate at least 1 hour or up to 8 hours, but return to room temperature before cooking.
2. Prepare a medium-hot fire in a covered charcoal or gas grill. Grill the lamb, turning occasionally and brushing often with the marinade, until the outside is nicely browned and the thickest part of the interior is medium-rare, about 20 to 25 minutes.

Garlic and Oregano Boneless Leg of Lamb

These heady, assertive flavors reminiscent of a Mediterranean summer are particularly well suited to grilled lamb. Most markets sell boneless leg of lamb these days, but if not, given a little notice, the butcher will be happy to bone and butterfly a shank or butt half for you.

6 Servings

---

3 pounds boned and butterflied leg of lamb

½ cup dry red wine

¼ cup olive oil

2 tablespoons Dijon mustard

6 garlic cloves, chopped

2 tablespoons chopped fresh oregano, plus 6 sprigs, or 2 teaspoons dried

¾ teaspoon freshly ground black pepper

---

1. Trim all excess fat from the lamb. In a shallow dish large enough to hold the lamb, whisk together the wine, olive oil, mustard, garlic, chopped oregano, and pepper. Add the lamb and turn to coat completely. Cover and refrigerate at least 4 hours or up to 24 hours, turning occasionally.

2. Prepare a medium-hot fire in a covered charcoal or gas grill. Remove the meat from the marinade and pat it dry, but leave any bits of garlic and oregano that cling on the meat. If using fresh oregano sprigs, dampen about half of them in water just before cooking, then toss them onto the hot coals.

3. Grill the lamb, turning once or twice, until the outside is nicely browned and the thickest part of the meat is at least medium-rare, a total of about 20 to 22 minutes. Remove the meat to a carving board and let it rest for a few minutes before carving into thin slices. Serve garnished with additional oregano sprigs, if you have them.

Spiced Rack of Lamb

Admittedly pricey, rack of lamb is beautiful to look at and a treat to eat.

4 Servings

---

2 racks of lamb (about 5 pounds total)
1½ teaspoons ground coriander
¾ teaspoon ground cumin
½ teaspoon ground cardamom
¼ teaspoon cinnamon

¼ teaspoon ground cloves
½ teaspoon salt
¼ teaspoon cayenne
2 tablespoons olive oil
1 garlic clove, minced

---

1. Trim all excess fat from the lamb, leaving a ⅛- to ¼-inch covering on the outside. In a small dish, blend together the coriander, cumin, cardamom, cinnamon, cloves, salt, and cayenne. In another small dish, combine the olive oil and garlic. Brush the garlic oil over the lamb. Season generously with the spice mixture, patting it on. Let stand 20 minutes or refrigerate up to 8 hours, but return to room temperature to cook.

2. Prepare a medium-hot fire in a covered charcoal or gas grill. Grill the racks of lamb, turning occasionally, until crispy and browned on the outside but still pink on the inside, about 17 to 20 minutes total. Let stand 5 to 10 minutes before carving.

Grilled Lamb Chops with Spicy Mint Pesto

A brief marinating time in a simple vinaigrette gives these chops a taste most complementary to the Spicy Mint Pesto that accompanies them.

4 Servings

¼ cup olive oil

3 tablespoons lemon juice

⅛ teaspoon salt

⅛ teaspoon freshly ground pepper

8 loin or rib lamb chops, cut about 1
  inch thick

Spicy Mint Pesto (recipe follows)

Fresh mint sprigs, for garnish

---

1. In a small dish, whisk together the olive oil, lemon juice, salt, and pepper. Brush all over the lamb, then let the chops stand at room temperature 30 minutes, or refrigerate up to 2 hours, but return to room temperature before cooking.

2. Prepare a medium-hot fire in a covered charcoal or gas grill. Grill the lamb, turning once, until browned on the outside but still pink on the inside, about 10 to 12 minutes.

3. Serve the chops topped with small spoonfuls of the Spicy Mint Pesto and garnished with mint sprigs.

Spicy Mint Pesto

Mint has a natural peppery undertone that is heightened by hot red pepper in this unconventional pesto that is good on all sorts of simple grilled lamb cuts. Blended with mayonnaise, sour cream, or yogurt, this sauce can be turned into a good dip for raw vegetables.

Makes about 1 cup

1 cup lightly packed fresh mint leaves	1 tablespoon lemon juice
⅔ cup lightly packed parsley sprigs	1 teaspoon grated lemon zest
⅓ cup grated Parmesan cheese	¼ teaspoon salt
¼ cup pine nuts	¼ teaspoon crushed hot red pepper
2 large garlic cloves, minced	⅓ cup extra-virgin olive oil

1. Place the mint, parsley, cheese, pine nuts, garlic, lemon juice, lemon zest, salt, and hot pepper in a food processor. Process, scraping the bowl once or twice, until a coarse puree forms. With the machine on, pour in the olive oil and process until the sauce is pureed, about 10 seconds.

2. Let the pesto stand at least 15 minutes at room temperature or refrigerate up to 24 hours, but return to room temperature to serve.

Lamb Steaks with Thai Hot and Sweet Sauce

Part of the popularity of Thai food is its wonderfully complex blend of hot and sweet flavors that tingle the taste buds. Here is a simplified take on a classic combination.

4 Servings

½ cup mint jelly

1 jalapeño pepper, seeded and minced

2 tablespoons lime juice

1 teaspoon grated lime zest

¼ cup chopped fresh basil, plus sprigs
   for garnish

8 lamb steaks or shoulder chops, cut
   about ½ inch thick

Salt and freshly ground pepper

---

1. In a small saucepan set over medium-low heat, melt the jelly with the jalapeño pepper, lime juice, and lime zest. Remove from the heat and stir in the chopped basil. Let the sauce stand at room temperature 30 minutes before using. (The sauce can be made several hours ahead. Reheat gently if it sets.) Remove and reserve ¼ cup of the sauce to use as a baste.

2. Prepare a medium-hot fire in a covered charcoal or gas grill. Season the lamb with salt and pepper. Grill, turning once, 2 minutes per side. Brush with the reserved ¼ cup sauce and grill, turning once and basting again, until browned on the outside but still pink on the inside, about 3 to 5 minutes longer.

3. Serve the lamb with the remaining sauce and garnished with the basil sprigs.

Curried Coconut Lamb Steaks

Cream of coconut is often sold in the beverage section of the market since it is a common ingredient in tropical drinks. Here it becomes a part of a simple West Indian-style marinade for lamb chops. Good-quality bottled chutney makes an attractive and tasty accompaniment.

4 Servings

---

1 cup canned cream of coconut

3 tablespoons lime juice

1 teaspoon grated lime zest

1 teaspoon curry powder

½ teaspoon salt

½ teaspoon freshly ground pepper

8 lamb steaks or shoulder chops, cut about ½ inch thick

¼ cup unsweetened toasted coconut (see Note below)

½ cup bottled chutney

4 thin slices of lime, for garnish

---

1. In a shallow dish just large enough to hold the lamb, combine the cream of coconut, lime juice, lime zest, curry powder, salt, and pepper. Add the lamb steaks and turn to coat completely. Cover and refrigerate at least 1 hour or up to 4 hours. Return to room temperature before cooking.

2. Prepare a hot fire in a covered charcoal or gas grill. Remove the lamb from the marinade and grill, turning once, until browned on the outside but still pink on the inside, about 7 to 9 minutes.

3. Serve the lamb chops sprinkled with the toasted coconut and with a spoonful of chutney to the side. Garnish each serving with a slice of lime.

NOTE: Unsweetened coconut is available at large markets, at Indian groceries, and in health food stores. Toast coconut on a small baking sheet in a preheated 350 degree oven, stirring often, until golden and fragrant, about 5 minutes.

Souvlaki with Cucumber-Yogurt Sauce

Souvlaki is a famous street snack, especially in central Greece, where vendors line the roads. When rolled or spooned into soft pita breads and served with the cooling thickened yogurt and cucumber sauce called tzatziki, *it becomes a substantial sandwich. It is traditional to use large flat pitas without pockets, but you can also spoon it into regular pita breads with pockets.*

4 main-course or 8 appetizer servings

¼ cup lemon juice
2 tablespoons extra-virgin olive oil
½ teaspoon dried oregano
1 garlic clove, chopped
¼ teaspoon salt
⅛ teaspoon freshly ground pepper
1 pound well-trimmed boneless leg of
lamb, cut into 1-inch cubes

Cucumber-Yogurt Sauce (recipe follows)
4 pita breads
2 tomatoes, coarsely chopped
1 small red onion, thinly sliced
2 cups shredded romaine lettuce

1. In a shallow dish just large enough to hold the lamb, combine the lemon juice, olive oil, oregano, garlic, salt, and pepper. Add the lamb and turn to coat completely. Refrigerate at least 2 hours or up to 12 hours.

2. Prepare a hot fire in a covered charcoal or gas grill. Thread the lamb onto metal skewers. Grill, turning occasionally and brushing with the marinade, until the lamb is richly browned on the outside and pink on the inside, about 5 minutes.

3. Spoon some of the Cucumber-Yogurt Sauce onto or into the pita breads, then remove the lamb from the skewers and place in the pitas. Add the tomatoes, onion, and lettuce. Pass any remaining sauce separately.

Cucumber-Yogurt Sauce

Thickening yogurt gives it all the texture of sour cream, but without any of the fat. This sauce makes a fabulous dip for fresh vegetables. It can also be served with grilled lamb or chicken. It is the traditional accompaniment to souvlaki.

Makes about 1½ cups

---

2 cups plain yogurt
1 small cucumber, seeded and coarsely
  chopped
Salt
3 tablespoons finely chopped scallion
  greens

2 tablespoons finely chopped parsley
2 tablespoons finely chopped fresh dill
  or 2 teaspoons dried
½ teaspoon sugar
¼ teaspoon freshly ground pepper

---

1. Spoon the yogurt into a cheesecloth-lined sieve and set over a bowl. Refrigerate 6 to 8 hours, then discard the liquid and place the thickened yogurt in a bowl.
2. Meanwhile, place the cucumber in another sieve or colander and sprinkle lightly with salt. Allow to drain for about 30 minutes. Rinse to remove the salt. Drain well; pat dry on a kitchen towel. Add the cucumber to the thickened yogurt. Stir in the scallion greens, parsley, dill, sugar, pepper, and salt to taste.
3. Cover and refrigerate 1 to 2 hours before using.

Lamb and Summer Vegetable Kebabs

Kebabs are great fun for family meals or entertaining. Meats and colorful vegetables on skewers are delicious and look terrific. It is most important to leave a little space in between each piece to encourage even cooking, and to use ingredients that will cook to optimum doneness at about the same time.

4 Servings

¼ cup olive oil
2 tablespoons red wine vinegar
2 garlic cloves, minced
¾ teaspoon ground cumin
½ teaspoon ground coriander
½ teaspoon cayenne
½ teaspoon salt

½ teaspoon freshly ground pepper
1 pound well-trimmed boneless leg of lamb, cut into 1½-inch cubes
1 medium zucchini, cut into 1-inch chunks
1 medium crookneck squash, cut into 1-inch chunks

1. In a shallow dish just large enough to hold the lamb, whisk together the olive oil, vinegar, garlic, cumin, coriander, cayenne, salt, and pepper. Add the lamb and turn to coat all over. Cover and refrigerate at least 1 hour or up to 8 hours. Return to room temperature before cooking.

2. Prepare a hot fire in a covered charcoal or gas grill. Remove the meat from the marinade and pat dry. Add the squash chunks to the marinade and toss to coat. Thread the meat and squash alternately onto metal skewers.

3. Grill, turning occasionally and brushing with marinade, until the lamb is nicely browned on the outside and pink on the inside and squash is tender and tinged with brown, about 7 to 8 minutes total.

Lamb and Rosemary Spiedini

Italians love these quickly grilled skewers of meat. They can be composed of all sorts of edibles, but lamb and sausages are typical, and the lemon wedge on the side is very traditional. Tossing rosemary branches onto the hot coals gives an extra boost of flavor.

4 Servings

⅓ cup olive oil
¼ cup balsamic vinegar
2 garlic cloves, minced
1½ tablespoons chopped fresh rosemary
  or 1 teaspoon dried
½ teaspoon salt
¼ teaspoon freshly ground pepper
1½ pounds well-trimmed boneless leg
  of lamb, cut in 1½-inch chunks

1 large sweet onion, cut into 1-inch
  chunks
1 lemon, cut into wedges

4 whole branches fresh rosemary,
  optional

1. In a shallow dish just large enough to hold the meat, combine the olive oil, vinegar, garlic, chopped rosemary, salt, and pepper. Add the lamb and stir to coat completely. Let stand 30 minutes or refrigerate up to 6 hours, but return to room temperature before cooking.

2. Prepare a hot fire in a covered charcoal or gas grill. Remove the lamb from the marinade and thread, along with the onion, onto 4 metal skewers. Brush the onion with the remaining marinade.

3. Just before cooking, dampen the rosemary branches and toss them onto the coals. Grill the spiedini, turning once or twice and brushing with any remaining marinade, until the lamb is nicely browned on the outside and medium-rare on the inside and the onion is crisp-tender, about 8 minutes total.

4. Serve directly from the skewers, with lemon wedges on the side.

Lamb and Melon Kebabs

Yogurt gives this lamb a richly browned crust and the sweet fruits a light, tangy contrast. Now that cut-up melon pieces can be purchased in the produce section and at the salad bar of supermarkets, you can use a couple of kinds to make this prettier and even more exotic. A couscous or rice salad dressed with lemon juice and olive oil would make the perfect accompaniment.

4 Servings

1 cup plain yogurt	¼ teaspoon cayenne
2 tablespoons orange juice	⅛ teaspoon ground cloves
¼ cup chopped fresh mint	1¼ pounds well-trimmed boneless leg
¾ teaspoon ground cumin	of lamb, cut into 1½-inch chunks
½ teaspoon ground coriander	3 cups assorted 1- to 1½-inch chunks
½ teaspoon salt	of melon, such as honeydew and
¼ teaspoon cinnamon	cantaloupe, but not watermelon

1. In a shallow dish just large enough to hold the meat, whisk together the yogurt, orange juice, mint, cumin, coriander, salt, cinnamon, cayenne, and cloves. Add the lamb and turn to coat all over. Cover and refrigerate at least 1 hour and up to 8 hours. Return to room temperature before cooking.

2. Prepare a medium-hot fire in a covered charcoal or gas grill. Remove the meat from the marinade and thread, along with the melon, on metal skewers, placing the melon near the ends to be away from the hottest heat. Brush the melon with some of the marinade.

3. Grill, turning occasionally and brushing with marinade, until the lamb is nicely browned on the outside and pink on the inside and melon is tinged with brown and just softened, about 7 to 8 minutes total.

Grilled Lamb Burgers in Pita Pockets

Here's a dish that's perfect if you feel like lamb for lunch. Alfalfa sprouts make a tasty filler, but any kind of sprout, watercress, or even shredded lettuce can be substituted.

4 Servings

---

1 pound lean ground lamb
½ cup chopped onion
½ cup fine fresh bread crumbs
2 tablespoons chopped fresh mint or
   1½ teaspoons dried
1 garlic clove, crushed through a press
1 teaspoon ground cumin
½ teaspoon ground coriander

½ teaspoon salt
½ teaspoon freshly ground pepper
4 whole wheat pita breads, partially
   split to make a pocket
½ cup plain yogurt
1 large tomato, seeded and diced
1 cup alfalfa sprouts

---

1. Prepare a hot fire in a covered charcoal or gas grill. In a large mixing bowl, blend together the ground lamb, onion, bread crumbs, mint, garlic, cumin, coriander, salt, and pepper. Form into 4 oval patties, each about 4½ inches long and ½ inch thick.

2. Grill, turning once, until well browned on the outside and barely pink in the center, about 8 to 10 minutes total. Just before the burgers are done, warm the pitas for about 1 minute at the edge of the grill.

3. Assemble the sandwiches by spreading the pockets of the pita breads lightly with some of the yogurt, then inserting a lamb patty. Garnish with diced tomato, sprouts, and the remaining yogurt.

Grilled Moroccan Lamb and Couscous Salad

Since most of the work can be done in advance, this salad is delightful for a summer party. It is a one-dish meal that needs only some warmed pita breads to round it out.

6 to 8 Servings

---

3 pounds boned and butterflied leg of
    lamb
½ cup dry red wine
2 tablespoons olive oil
2 teaspoons dried marjoram

½ teaspoon salt
½ teaspoon freshly ground pepper
1 head of romaine lettuce
Couscous Salad (recipe follows)
2 tomatoes, cut into wedges

---

1. Trim all excess fat from the lamb. In a shallow dish large enough to hold the lamb, combine the wine, olive oil, marjoram, salt, and pepper. Add the lamb and turn to coat all over. Cover and refrigerate at least 4 hours or up to 24 hours, turning occasionally. Return to room temperature before cooking.

2. Prepare a medium-hot fire in a covered charcoal or gas grill. Remove the lamb from the marinade and blot it dry with paper toweling. Grill the lamb, turning once or twice, until the outside is nicely browned and the interior is medium-rare, about 15 to 20 minutes total. Let the meat rest 3 to 5 minutes, then carve into thin slices.

3. To assemble the salad, arrange romaine leaves on a large platter or individual plates. Spoon on a mound of couscous, arrange the warm lamb over the top, and garnish with tomato wedges.

Couscous Salad with Mint Vinaigrette

This is a terrific pairing with grilled lamb, but it can also stand alone or in combination with grilled chicken or beef. Because there is no mayonnaise, the salad transports well and is a wonderful picnic dish. Couscous, a tiny North African pasta, is widely available in the rice sections of large supermarkets.

6 to 8 Servings

---

2 cups couscous
3 cups boiling water
1 teaspoon salt
1 green bell pepper, cut into ¼- to ½-inch dice
1 yellow or red bell pepper, cut into ¼- to ½-inch dice
¾ cup chopped red onion

1 cup packed parsley sprigs
1 cup packed mint sprigs
2 garlic cloves, crushed through a press
¼ cup lemon juice
1 tablespoon Dijon mustard
¾ cup olive oil
½ teaspoon freshly ground pepper

---

1. Place the couscous in a large mixing bowl. Add the boiling water and ½ teaspoon of the salt. Cover the bowl tightly with a lid or aluminum foil and let the couscous stand until the liquid is absorbed, 5 to 7 minutes. Uncover and add the green and yellow peppers and the onion. Toss with a fork to combine and fluff the couscous.

2. In a food processor, coarsely chop the parsley, mint, and garlic. With the machine on, pour in the lemon juice, mustard, and olive oil, and process just until blended. Season with the remaining ½ teaspoon salt and the pepper. Pour the vinaigrette over the couscous and toss to mix. (The salad can be prepared about 4 hours ahead and refrigerated. Return to cool room temperature before serving.)

Chapter Six
Fish and Shellfish

Grilling is the way to convert meat eaters to seafood lovers. The grill seems to bring out the best in fish and shellfish while adding a flavor distinctively different from seafood cooked any other way. At our house, one of our sons always requests grilled fish steaks for his birthday dinner.

The best fish for grilling are those that are firm fleshed, such as salmon, swordfish, tuna, halibut, shark, mahimahi, grouper, trout, and snapper. Flakier, more delicate fillets, such as sole, tend to fall apart and are overwhelmed by the charcoal flavor, so are better cooked indoors. Whole fish can be grilled using a specially hinged fish grill that makes turning them easier.

Shellfish take well to grilling, especially as brochettes that can be turned easily. Clams and oysters can be cooked in the shell, but scallops and shrimp do best on skewers, which prevent the small pieces from falling through the grill grate. Shrimp, which tend to curl and cook unevenly, can be easily handled if the dual skewer method is used. Simply thread the shrimp onto two parallel metal or soaked bamboo skewers, the fatter ends through one and the tails through the other. This keeps the shrimp flat for even cooking, easy turning, and attractive presentation.

Seafood should be cooked over hot or medium-hot coals just until done: that is, until white and opaque in the center. Watch carefully to prevent overcooking and drying out. Because seafood is so low in fat, the grill rack should always be oiled before cooking.

Grilled Catfish with Cornmeal and Pecan Crust

Steamed green beans and stewed tomatoes would round out this delicate, Southern-style seafood treatment. Other firm fish fillets, such as grouper or mahimahi, can be substituted for the catfish.

4 Servings

¾ cup yellow cornmeal
⅓ cup finely chopped pecans
½ teaspoon salt
¼ teaspoon freshly ground pepper
½ cup milk

2 teaspoons lemon juice
¾ teaspoon Tabasco or other hot sauce
4 catfish fillets (about 6 ounces each)
Tartar sauce and lemon wedges

1. On a plate, combine the cornmeal, pecans, salt, and pepper. Mix well. In a shallow dish just large enough to hold the fish, combine the milk, lemon juice, and Tabasco sauce. Place the fish in the milk mixture and turn to coat completely. Let stand for 10 minutes or cover and refrigerate for up to 30 minutes.

2. Remove the fish from the liquid and dredge in the cornmeal mixture to coat the fillets completely. Place the fish in a single layer on a baking sheet. Refrigerate at least 10 minutes or up to 1 hour.

3. Prepare a medium fire in a covered charcoal or gas grill. Oil the grill rack. Grill the fish until the coating is golden brown on one side, about 4 to 5 minutes. Carefully turn the fish with a wide spatula and grill until the other side is golden brown and the fish is just cooked through, 4 to 5 minutes longer. Serve with tartar sauce and lemon wedges.

Grilled Mahimahi with Toasted Coconut and Macadamia Butter

Mahimahi, also known as dolphin steak, is a mildly flavored firm Pacific fish. Halibut steaks are a good substitute if you can't get mahimahi. The fish is excellent without the flavored butter, but it does add a festive touch for entertaining.

6 Servings

¼ cup plus 2 tablespoons shredded coconut

¼ cup plus 2 tablespoons coarsely chopped macadamia nuts

4 tablespoons unsalted butter, softened

1 teaspoon grated orange zest

⅓ cup orange juice

⅓ cup soy sauce

1 tablespoon vegetable oil

½ teaspoon curry powder

6 skinless mahimahi fillets, cut 1 inch thick (about 2 pounds total)

---

1. Preheat the oven to 350 degrees. Place the coconut and macadamia nuts in separate areas on a baking sheet. Toast, stirring often, until coconut and nuts are golden and fragrant, about 6 minutes. Let cool. In a small bowl, blend together ¼ cup each of the toasted coconut and nuts with the butter and orange zest. (The flavored butter can be made 2 days ahead and refrigerated. Return to room temperature before using.)

2. In a shallow dish just large enough to hold the fish, combine the orange juice, soy sauce, oil, and curry powder. Add the fish and turn to coat both sides. Let marinate 30 minutes.

3. Prepare a hot fire in a covered charcoal or gas grill. Oil the grill rack. Grill the fish, turning once, until just cooked through, about 10 minutes.

4. Serve the fish topped with the flavored butter and sprinkled with the remaining toasted coconut and macadamia nuts.

Grilled Mackerel with Romesco Sauce

Mackerel is a strong-flavored fish that is especially delicious when very, very fresh. Bluefish fillets are a good substitute. Both are firm textured and thus take well to grilling. Romesco sauce, with its assertive flavor, is a fine partner for the mackerel.

6 Servings

---

2 tablespoons lemon juice	¼ teaspoon freshly ground pepper
2 tablespoons olive oil	2 pounds mackerel fillets
½ teaspoon salt	Romesco Sauce (recipe follows)

---

1. In a shallow dish just large enough to hold the fish, combine the lemon juice, olive oil, salt, and pepper. Add the fish and turn to coat both sides. Let stand 30 minutes.

2. Prepare a hot fire in a covered charcoal or gas grill. Set the fish skin side up on the grill. Grill, turning once with a wide spatula, until the fish is just cooked through, about 8 to 10 minutes total.

3. Serve the fish fillets with the Romesco Sauce spooned on top.

Romesco Sauce

The vegetables for this sauce from the Catalan region of Spain are usually roasted, then mashed together. Here the tomatoes, peppers, and bread are grilled to give even more depth to this fabulous sauce, which is also wonderful on grilled chicken or steak. Purists might make this with a mortar and pestle, but I use a food processor.

Makes about 1½ cups

¼ cup plus 2 tablespoons slivered
  almonds
2 garlic cloves, peeled
1 red bell pepper, halved
1 small Italian frying pepper, halved
1 large tomato, halved and seeded

1 slice of French bread, about ¾ inch
  thick
¼ teaspoon cayenne
2 tablespoons dry red or white wine
1 tablespoon sherry wine vinegar
¼ cup olive oil
Salt

---

1. In a frying pan set over medium heat, stir the almonds until they are golden brown and fragrant, about 3 minutes. Remove immediately from the pan to prevent further cooking, then cool to room temperature. (The nuts can be toasted a day ahead and stored in a tightly covered container.)

2. Prepare a medium-hot fire in a covered charcoal or gas grill. Oil the grill rack. Wrap the garlic cloves in heavy-duty aluminum foil to make a small packet. Set at the side of the grill and roast until the garlic is softened and barely tinged with brown, about 15 minutes. Grill the red and frying peppers over the center of the fire, turning often, until the peppers are softened and the skin is blackened, about 8 to 10 minutes. Place the peppers in a paper bag and let cool 10 minutes. Meanwhile, grill the tomato in the center of the grill, turning occasionally with a spatula until the skin is lightly browned and the tomato begins to soften, about 5 to 7 minutes. Grill the bread on the edges of the grill, turning once, until lightly toasted on both sides, about 3 minutes total.

3. Peel the garlic, peppers, and tomatoes. Tear the toasted bread into pieces. Place the almonds, garlic, peppers, tomatoes, bread, cayenne, wine, and vinegar in a food processor. Pulse until all the ingredients are chopped but not pureed. With the machine on, pour the olive oil through the feed tube to make a coarse puree.

4. Season the sauce to taste with salt. Let stand for at least 30 minutes or up to 4 hours before serving.

Grilled Monkfish Chowder

Admittedly, this is a loose interpretation of a New England classic, but even my most stalwart Yankee friends love it. Pilot or chowder crackers are still the best accompaniment. If you are entertaining real traditionalists, serve Boston cream pie for dessert.

6 Servings

---

12 slices of bacon

1 pound small red potatoes (about 1½ inches in diameter)

1½ pounds monkfish fillets, cut into 24 (1½-inch) chunks

2 teaspoons dried thyme leaves

1 large onion, cut into 1½-inch chunks

4 cups light cream or half-and-half

1 cup bottled clam juice

½ teaspoon freshly ground pepper

Salt

¼ cup chopped parsley

---

1. In a large frying pan, partially cook the bacon over medium heat so that it renders some of the fat but is still limp, about 3 minutes. Drain and cut each bacon slice in half. Boil the potatoes in a large saucepan of salted water until almost fork-tender, about 5 minutes. Season the fish with 1 teaspoon of the thyme, then wrap each fish chunk in a piece of bacon. Skewer the bacon-wrapped fish, potatoes, and onion chunks onto separate metal skewers.

2. Prepare a medium fire in a covered charcoal or gas grill. Oil the grill rack. Grill the fish, potatoes, and onions, turning occasionally, until the fish is cooked through, the bacon is crisp, and the onions are tender, 10 to 12 minutes.

---

3. While the fish is grilling, in a medium saucepan, bring the cream, clam juice, pepper, and remaining 1 teaspoon thyme to a simmer. Season with salt to taste. Keep warm over low heat.

4. To serve, transfer the fish, potatoes, and onions from the skewers to 6 shallow soup bowls. Pour the heated cream mixture over the fish and garnish with chopped parsley.

Grilled Salmon Cakes with Caper Crème Fraîche

Though they can also be made with cod, these cakes are particularly nice with salmon, which lends its lovely pink color to the finished dish. If you have fresh dill, use some sprigs as garnish. The fishmonger will skin and bone the salmon for you.

6 Servings

1 cup crème fraîche (see Note below)
3 tablespoons drained small capers
1 tablespoon grated lemon zest
1½ pounds skinless, boneless salmon
  fillets
1½ cups fresh white bread crumbs
¼ cup chopped chives

3 tablespoons chopped fresh dill or 1
  tablespoon dried
2 tablespoons Dijon mustard
2 tablespoons lemon juice
¾ teaspoon freshly ground pepper
½ teaspoon salt
1 egg, beaten
6 lemon wedges

1. In a small bowl, stir together the crème fraîche, capers, and 1 teaspoon of the lemon zest. Cover and refrigerate for at least 1 hour and up to 4 hours, but return to room temperature before serving.
2. Cut the salmon into roughly 1-inch chunks. Working in 2 batches, pulse the salmon in a food processor until it is coarsely chopped; do not puree to a paste. In a large mixing bowl, use your hands to blend the chopped salmon with 1 cup of the bread crumbs, the chives, dill, mustard, lemon juice, pepper, salt, egg, and remaining 2 teaspoons lemon zest.

3. Divide the mixture into 6 portions and form each into a patty about ¾ inch thick. Place the remaining ½ cup bread crumbs on a plate and dredge the patties in the crumbs to coat all over, pressing gently with your hands to help them adhere. Refrigerate the patties in a single layer for 30 minutes.

4. Prepare a hot fire in a covered charcoal or gas grill. Oil the grill rack. Grill the salmon patties, turning once carefully with a wide spatula, until the salmon is just cooked through and the patties are lightly browned, about 8 minutes total.

5. Serve the salmon topped with spoonfuls of the flavored crème fraîche and garnished with lemon wedges.

NOTE: If you can't find crème fraîche in your market, you can make your own by stirring 1 tablespoon sour cream into 1 cup heavy cream. Cover and let stand at room temperature until it is thickened, about 24 hours. Refrigerate up to a week. Or you can substitute plain yogurt and save on the fat as well as the work.

Grilled Mustard-Dill Salmon Roast

A whole piece of salmon cooked as a roast makes a very pretty presentation, but individual salmon steaks or fillets can also be used, adjusting the cooking time to about 5 minutes per side.

6 Servings

¼ cup lemon juice
¼ cup Dijon mustard
¼ cup olive oil
3 tablespoons minced shallots
½ cup chopped fresh dill
½ teaspoon freshly ground pepper

2½ to 3 pounds side of salmon fillet, in one piece
1 cup plain yogurt or sour cream
1 tablespoon grated lemon zest
Whole dill sprigs, for garnish

---

1. In a shallow dish just large enough to hold the fish, whisk together the lemon juice, mustard, olive oil, shallots, chopped dill, and pepper to blend well. Add the salmon and turn to coat both sides. Cover and refrigerate at least 30 minutes and up to 3 hours. Return to room temperature before cooking.

2. Combine the yogurt with the lemon zest. Refrigerate until ready to use.

3. Prepare a medium fire in a covered charcoal or gas grill. Cover and grill the salmon, skin side down, until nicely browned on the bottom, about 10 minutes. Carefully turn over with 1 or 2 wide spatulas and grill until the fish is just opaque throughout, 5 to 10 minutes longer.

4. Serve the fish garnished with dill sprigs and accompanied by the lemon yogurt sauce.

Blackened Red Snapper Fillets

You can use other firm fish fillets, such as redfish, grouper, or catfish, in this recipe with equally good results. Cool the heat of the Creole coating with a side dish of creamy coleslaw.

4 Servings

1½ tablespoons chili powder
1 tablespoon paprika
1 teaspoon salt
1 teaspoon dried onion powder
1 teaspoon dried garlic powder
½ teaspoon ground cumin

½ teaspoon cayenne
½ teaspoon freshly ground black
  pepper
4 red snapper fillets (about 6 ounces
  each)
Lemon wedges

1. In a small dish, mix together the chili powder, paprika, salt, onion powder, garlic powder, cumin, cayenne, and black pepper.

2. Prepare a medium fire in a covered charcoal or gas grill. Oil the grill rack. Sprinkle both sides of the fish with the spice mixture, patting it in lightly with your fingertips.

3. Cover and grill the fish, skin side down, for 4 minutes. Turn and grill until the fish is just opaque throughout, about 4 minutes longer. Serve with lemon wedges.

Grilled Swordfish Siciliana

Swordfish is as popular for grilling in Sicily as it is here, probably because the meaty texture and full flavor marry well with the piquant seasonings of that region of Italy.

4 Servings

⅔ cup dry white wine

3 tablespoons olive oil

2 teaspoons dried oregano

1½ pounds swordfish steaks, cut about ¾ inch thick

Salt and freshly ground pepper

2 garlic cloves, crushed through a press

4 anchovy fillets, chopped

¾ pound fresh plum tomatoes, seeded and coarsely chopped

¼ cup chopped flat-leaf parsley

1 tablespoon drained small capers

2 teaspoons lemon juice

1 teaspoon grated lemon zest

---

1. In a shallow dish just large enough to hold the fish, combine ⅓ cup of the wine, 2 tablespoons of the olive oil, and 1 teaspoon of the oregano. Lightly season the fish with salt and pepper. Add the fish to the marinade and turn to coat both sides. Let stand 30 minutes or refrigerate up to 2 hours, turning occasionally.

2. Meanwhile, in a medium frying pan, heat the remaining 1 tablespoon olive oil and cook the garlic over medium-low heat until softened and fragrant, about 1 minute. Add the anchovies and mash them with the back of a spoon. Add the tomatoes, remaining ⅓ cup wine, and remaining 1 teaspoon oregano. Bring to a boil and cook, stirring often, until the liquid is reduced by half, about 4 minutes.

3. Stir in the parsley, capers, lemon juice, and lemon zest. Simmer 2 minutes. Season with salt and pepper to taste. Keep the sauce warm over very low heat or serve at room temperature.

4. Prepare a medium-hot fire in a covered charcoal or gas grill. Oil the grill rack. Grill the fish, turning once with a wide spatula, until lightly browned outside and just opaque to the center but still moist, about 8 to 10 minutes. Serve the fish with the tomato sauce ladled over it.

Grilled Seafood Brochettes on Pesto Pasta

It's just as easy, and a lot more interesting, to buy two kinds of fish for these brochettes. Ask the fishmonger for the end or other odd pieces, which are usually less expensive than fish steaks. You can make your own pesto if you have a basil patch, but there are several good refrigerated commercial brands on the market today, so this summery dish can be enjoyed even in the dead of winter.

4 Servings

---

2 tablespoons olive oil
2 tablespoons lemon juice
½ teaspoon freshly ground pepper
½ pound swordfish chunks or steaks, about 1 inch thick

½ pound tuna chunks or steak, about 1 inch thick
1 pound thin linguine or spaghettini
1 cup pesto sauce
¼ cup dry white wine

---

1. In a shallow dish just large enough to hold the fish, combine the olive oil, lemon juice, and pepper. Add the swordfish and tuna chunks and turn to coat all over. Let stand at room temperature for 30 minutes or refrigerate for up to 2 hours.
2. Prepare a hot fire in a covered charcoal or gas grill. Bring a large pot of salted water to a boil. Thread the fish onto metal skewers.
3. Add the pasta to the boiling water and cook until tender but still firm, 7 to 9 minutes; drain. Meanwhile, grill the skewered fish, turning occasionally, until just cooked through, about 8 to 10 minutes.
4. Toss the hot pasta with the pesto sauce and the wine. Spoon onto a platter or serving plates. Remove the fish from the skewers and arrange on top of the pasta. Serve at once.

Grilled Rainbow Trout Stuffed with Citrus and Cilantro

This is as pretty a dish as it is tasty. Because of the increase in farm-raised fish, small boned trout are widely available at fish markets these days, but you could use the same stuffing and cooking method for small coho salmon, too.

4 Servings

---

4 boned whole fresh trout (about 10 ounces each)
2 tablespoons olive oil
Salt and freshly ground pepper
8 thin orange slices

8 thin lemon slices
8 thin lime slices
¼ cup chopped fresh cilantro or parsley, plus sprigs for garnish

---

1. Prepare a medium fire in a covered charcoal or gas grill. Oil the grill rack.

2. Brush the trout inside and out with the olive oil. Season with salt and pepper. Laying the trout open, overlap 1 each of the orange, lemon, and lime slices along one side. Sprinkle each with 1 tablespoon of the chopped cilantro, then fold the trout over to enclose the filling. Secure the opening with small skewers or wooden toothpicks.

3. Grill the trout for 5 minutes. Use a wide spatula to turn it carefully. Grill 4 to 5 minutes longer, until just cooked through. Serve garnished with the remaining citrus slices and cilantro sprigs.

Grill-Smoked Trout

I learned how to smoke trout during many years of fishing the mountain streams in western North Carolina. We smoked our freshly caught rainbows in a real smoker, but I developed an equally good method for the traditional grill I had at home. Though I now have a smoker at home and often use it for the fish, this grill-smoking does justice to your own catch, whether off the hook or from the local fish market. If you buy them, by all means, ask your fishmonger to bone them for you. Serve the fish with crackers as an appetizer or a light main course accompanied by a cucumber salad and boiled potatoes.

4 appetizer or 2 main-course servings

---

2 whole 10- to 12-ounce fresh trout, boned and butterflied

¼ cup coarse sea salt or kosher salt

Parsley sprigs, for garnish

2 or 3 handfuls hickory chips

---

1. Rinse the trout in cold water. In a large bowl or crock, dissolve the salt in about 2 quarts of water. Add the trout and additional water to cover them, if necessary. Cover the bowl and refrigerate the trout for 24 hours. (The fish will firm up in the brine.)

2. Soak the hickory chips in water to cover for at least 30 minutes. Prepare a medium fire in a covered charcoal grill, then push the hot coals to the side. Or prepare an indirect fire in a charcoal grill according to the manufacturer's directions. Oil the grill rack. Remove the fish from the brine, rinse under cold water, and pat dry on paper towels.

3. Just before cooking, toss the wet hickory chips onto the hot coals or add to a gas grill according to the manufacturer's instructions. Place the trout, skin side down, on the side of the grill away from the coals. Smoke for 40 minutes without turning and without opening the lid.

4. Present the whole trout on a platter, garnished with parsley sprigs.

Grilled Tuna and Japanese Eggplant on Soba Noodles

The simple but exotic vinaigrette prepared here doubles as a marinade for the tuna and as a sauce for the noodles. If you can't find soba (buckwheat) noodles, use thin spaghetti or spaghettini. The pasta can be cooked ahead and served at room temperature. If the small, narrow, deep purple Japanese eggplants aren't available, use an equal weight of regular eggplant, sliced about ¾ inch thick.

4 Servings

½ cup plus 1 tablespoon peanut oil
¼ cup plus 2 tablespoons rice wine
  vinegar
¼ cup finely chopped fresh ginger
4 garlic cloves, crushed through a
  press
2 tablespoons soy sauce
2 tablespoons hot chili sesame oil
2 tablespoons toasted sesame seeds (see
  Note below)

1 pound tuna steaks, cut about 1 inch
  thick
2 narrow Japanese eggplants, halved
  lengthwise (about ¾ pound total)
1 (8½-ounce) package soba (buckwheat) noodles, cooked and drained
  according to package directions
½ cup thinly sliced scallions

1. In a small bowl, whisk together ½ cup of the peanut oil with the vinegar, ginger, garlic, soy sauce, hot sesame oil, and sesame seeds. Remove 3 tablespoons of the vinaigrette to a shallow dish just large enough to hold the tuna. Reserve the remaining vinaigrette. Cut the tuna into 1-inch chunks and add to the dish, turning to coat all over. Let stand 30 minutes.

2. Prepare a hot fire in a covered charcoal or gas grill. Thread the tuna onto metal skewers or bamboo skewers that have been soaked for at least 30 minutes in cold water. Brush the cut sides of the eggplant with the remaining 1 tablespoon of peanut oil.

3. Grill the tuna kebabs and the eggplant halves, turning occasionally, until the tuna is just cooked through and the eggplant is tender, about 8 to 10 minutes total.

4. Toss the noodles and scallions with the remaining vinaigrette. Arrange on a platter or on serving plates. Top with tuna chunks and eggplant halves.

NOTE: Toast sesame seeds by tossing them in a small skillet over medium heat until golden and fragrant, about 3 minutes. Remove immediately from the skillet to prevent burning.

Grilled Tuna Salad Niçoise

This is a really special salad worthy of your best guests. All of the components can be made in advance, with the grilling of the fish and vegetables the only last-minute task. Be sure to offer a basket of crusty French rolls to complete the course.

6 Servings

¼ cup red or white wine vinegar

2 garlic cloves, crushed through a press

2 teaspoons chopped fresh savory or ¾ teaspoon dried

2 teaspoons chopped fresh rosemary or ½ teaspoon dried

¼ teaspoon crushed hot red pepper

½ cup plus 2 tablespoons extra-virgin olive oil

1½ pounds tuna steaks, cut about ¾ inch thick

1 pound small red potatoes

¾ pound slim green beans, trimmed

1 head of romaine lettuce, separated into leaves

1 red onion, thinly sliced

1 (2-ounce) can flat anchovy fillets

1 large tomato, cut into wedges

3 hard-boiled eggs, quartered

⅓ cup Niçoise olives

2 or 3 handfuls grapevine cuttings, optional

---

1. In a small bowl, whisk together the vinegar, garlic, savory, rosemary, and hot pepper. Whisk in the olive oil. Remove about ⅓ cup of the vinaigrette to a shallow dish just large enough to hold the tuna; reserve the remaining vinaigrette. Add the tuna and turn to coat all over. Cover and refrigerate at least 1 hour and up to 4 hours.

2. In a large saucepan of boiling salted water, cook the potatoes until just fork-tender, about 8 minutes. Remove with a slotted spoon and let cool. Add the beans to the boiling water and cook until just tender, about 3 minutes. Drain and rinse the beans under cold running water to cool; drain well. (The potatoes and the beans can be cooked several hours ahead and kept cool.)

3. If using grapevine cuttings, soak them in cold water for at least 30 minutes. Prepare a hot fire in a covered charcoal or gas grill. Oil the grill rack. Just before cooking, toss the cuttings onto the coals. Thread the potatoes onto skewers. Grill the tuna steaks and skewered potatoes, turning occasionally, until the tuna is cooked through and the potatoes are lightly browned, about 10 minutes total.

4. To assemble the salad, cut the tuna into ½-inch slices. On a large platter or on 6 serving plates, make a bed of the romaine leaves. Arrange the potatoes, tuna, green beans, and sliced onions on top in separate sections. Crisscross the anchovies over the tuna. Drizzle the remaining vinaigrette over the salad. Garnish the platter with the tomato wedges, egg quarters, and olives.

Grilled Crab Cakes with Spicy Mayonnaise

The best recipe for crab cakes is a hotly debated topic throughout Maryland, but everyone agrees that top-quality lump crabmeat is of greatest importance. True, but I have been known to make these with good canned crab and have never had any complaints or any leftovers, either.

4 Servings

½ cup plus 3 tablespoons mayonnaise

1 tablespoon plus 2 teaspoons lemon juice

½ to ¾ teaspoon Tabasco or other hot sauce

1 whole egg

1 egg white

3½ cups fresh white bread crumbs

⅓ cup finely chopped scallions

1 teaspoon Worcestershire sauce

¾ teaspoon Old Bay or other seafood seasoning blend

¾ teaspoon dry mustard

¼ teaspoon cayenne

12 to 16 ounces lump crabmeat, picked over, or 2 (6½-ounce) cans crabmeat, drained and picked over

2 tablespoons butter, melted

1. To make the sauce, stir together ½ cup of the mayonnaise, 1 tablespoon of the lemon juice, and the Tabasco until well blended. Cover and refrigerate for up to 2 days before using.

2. In a mixing bowl, whisk the whole egg with the egg white until blended. Add 2 cups of the bread crumbs, the scallions, the remaining 3 tablespoons mayonnaise, the remaining 2 teaspoons lemon juice, Worcestershire, Old Bay seasoning, mustard, and cayenne. Mix with your hands to blend well. Add the crabmeat and mix gently.

3. Form the crab mixture into 8 cakes, each about 3 inches in diameter. In a shallow bowl, toss the remaining 1½ cups bread crumbs with the melted butter. Dip the crab cakes into the buttered bread crumbs to coat completely. Place the crab cakes on a baking sheet in a single layer and refrigerate about 30 minutes or up to 2 hours to set the coating.

4. Prepare a medium fire in a covered charcoal or gas grill. Oil the grill rack. Grill the crab cakes, carefully turning once with a wide spatula, until lightly browned and with grill marks on both sides, about 8 minutes total. Serve the crab cakes with the spicy mayonnaise.

Grilled Soft-Shell Crabs with Mustard Butter

On the eastern shore of Maryland, eating crabs is an art form, especially during the spring and early summer when soft-shells are in season. There are lots of ways to cook these delicacies, but one of the easiest and best is grilling. The crabs, which are available at quality fish markets, should not be cleaned until you are ready to purchase them. If you have never had soft-shell crabs, remember that the shells themselves are edible, too.

6 Servings

---

4 tablespoons unsalted butter	½ teaspoon freshly ground pepper
3 tablespoons grainy Dijon mustard	12 fresh soft-shell crabs, cleaned

---

1. Prepare a medium-hot fire in a covered charcoal or gas grill. Oil the grill rack.
2. In a small saucepan, cook the butter over medium-low heat until it melts, just begins to brown, and smells nutty. Immediately remove from the heat and whisk in the mustard and pepper. Liberally brush the mustard butter all over the crabs.
3. Grill the crabs, back side down, until lightly browned, about 3 to 5 minutes. Brush with more mustard butter, turn, and grill on the other side until lightly browned and cooked through, about 3 to 5 minutes longer. Serve with any remaining mustard butter drizzled on top.

Grilled Shrimp Español

The highly seasoned marinade is boiled to use as a sauce for the grilled shrimp. Swordfish chunks can be treated the same way, or you can make a combination of fish and shellfish for a pretty party dish.

4 to 6 Servings

¾ cup dry sherry

½ cup olive oil

3 tablespoons lemon juice

8 garlic cloves, crushed through a press

½ teaspoon coarsely ground black pepper

⅛ teaspoon cayenne

1½ pounds shelled and deveined large shrimp

2 tablespoons chopped parsley

---

1. In a shallow dish just large enough to hold the shrimp, combine the sherry, olive oil, lemon juice, garlic, pepper, and cayenne. Add the shrimp and turn to coat completely. Let stand for 30 minutes.

2. Prepare a hot fire in a covered charcoal or gas grill. Thread the shrimp onto single or double skewers. Pour the marinade into a small saucepan and boil 3 minutes.

3. Grill the shrimp, turning once, until they are pink and firm to the touch, about 4 to 6 minutes total. Slide the shrimp off the skewers onto a platter. Pour the sauce over the shrimp. Garnish with the parsley and serve.

Grilled Shrimp and Sausage Jambalaya

This is a simplified interpretation of jambalaya in which skewered grilled shrimp and sausage are presented over a bed of colorful spicy rice. With a green salad and some French bread, it makes an impressive, easy meal for entertaining. Andouille is a garlicky Creole smoked sausage; quality kielbasa is a fine substitute.

6 Servings

3 tablespoons olive oil
1 cup dry white wine
1½ teaspoons dried thyme leaves
½ teaspoon cayenne
1 pound large shrimp, shelled and deveined
1 medium onion, chopped
1 green bell pepper, chopped
1 large celery rib, chopped

2 garlic cloves, crushed through a press
1 cup long-grain white rice
½ pound andouille or kielbasa sausage, cut into ½-inch slices
1 (16-ounce) can tomatoes in juice
⅔ cup bottled clam juice
½ to 1 teaspoon Tabasco sauce
¼ cup chopped parsley

1. In a shallow dish just large enough to hold the shrimp, combine 1 tablespoon of the olive oil, ½ cup of the wine, ½ teaspoon of the thyme, and ¼ teaspoon of the cayenne. Add the shrimp and turn to coat. Let stand 30 minutes or refrigerate up to 2 hours.

2. In a 12-inch frying pan with a lid or in a large flameproof casserole, heat the remaining 2 tablespoons olive oil. Add the onion, bell pepper, celery, and garlic and cook over medium heat until the vegetables are softened, about 3 minutes. Stir in the remaining 1 teaspoon thyme, ¼ teaspoon cayenne, and the rice. Cook, stirring, until the rice is opaque and the grains are coated with oil, about 1 minute.

Fish and Shellfish

Stir in the remaining ½ cup wine, the tomatoes with their juices, and the clam juice. Cover the pan and bring to a boil. Lower the heat to a simmer and cook until the rice is tender and the liquid is absorbed, about 25 minutes.

3. While the rice is cooking, prepare a hot fire in a covered charcoal or gas grill. Thread the shrimp and sausage onto 6 metal skewers or bamboo skewers that have been soaked at least 30 minutes in cold water. Grill, turning occasionally, until the shrimp are pink and firm to the touch and the sausage is browned, about 4 to 6 minutes total.

4. Season the cooked rice with Tabasco and stir in the parsley. Spread the rice on a platter or serving plate and top with the skewered shrimp and sausage.

Grilled Shrimp with Low Country Dipping Sauce

This sauce is inspired by traditional Carolina low country shrimp boils. Leave the tails on the shrimp to use as "dippers." When skewering shrimp for grilling, if you use two parallel metal or bamboo skewers, they will keep the shrimp flat so that they won't flip around when you turn them on the grill.

4 to 6 Servings

2 tablespoons olive oil	¾ cup dry white wine
2 tablespoons lemon juice	¾ cup bottled clam juice
¼ teaspoon freshly ground pepper	3 tablespoons butter
1½ pounds shelled and deveined large shrimp, with tails intact	2 teaspoons Old Bay or other seafood seasoning blend

1. In a shallow dish just large enough to hold the shrimp, combine the olive oil, lemon juice, and pepper. Add the shrimp and turn to coat completely. Let stand 30 minutes. In a small saucepan, heat the wine, clam juice, butter, and Old Bay seasoning over low heat until the butter melts. Keep warm.

2. Prepare a hot fire in a covered charcoal or gas grill. Thread the shrimp through the middle onto single or double skewers. Grill, turning once, until the shrimp are pink and firm to the touch, about 4 to 6 minutes total.

3. Slide the shrimp off the skewers onto a platter. Serve with the warm dipping sauce in a small bowl.

Grilled Shrimp and Sea Scallops on Pasta

Here the marinade becomes the basis for a terrific pasta sauce in this grilled version of a favorite treatment for shrimp.

4 Servings

¼ cup olive oil

3 garlic cloves, minced

3 tablespoons minced shallots

¾ cup dry white wine

¾ cup bottled clam juice

1½ teaspoons dried oregano

½ teaspoon crushed hot red pepper

¾ pound large shrimp, shelled and deveined

½ pound sea scallops

1 pound linguine

½ cup chopped flat-leaf parsley

1. In a large frying pan, combine the olive oil, garlic, shallots, wine, clam juice, oregano, and hot pepper. Add the shrimp and scallops and turn to coat all over. Let stand 15 minutes or refrigerate up to 1 hour.

2. Prepare a medium-hot fire in a covered charcoal or gas grill. Bring a large pot of water to a boil for the pasta. Thread the shrimp and scallops onto metal skewers. In a small nonaluminum saucepan, bring the reserved marinade to a simmer over medium-low heat. Simmer 5 minutes.

3. Add the pasta to the boiling water and cook until tender but still firm, 8 to 10 minutes. While the pasta is cooking, grill the shrimp and scallops, turning once or twice, until cooked through, 8 to 10 minutes.

4. To serve, drain the pasta and toss with the simmered marinade and the parsley. Spoon the pasta onto a platter and arrange the grilled shellfish on top.

Green Sea Scallop and Pineapple Kebabs

This is a delicate and very pretty main course for entertaining. Try to get sea scallops of uniform size, preferably about 1 inch, so that they will cook in about the same time. To save time, you can buy fresh pineapple cut in chunks from the salad bar at your grocery store.

4 Servings

1 bunch of fresh spinach	1 pound sea scallops (about 20)
3 tablespoons olive oil	2 cups 1½-inch chunks fresh pineapple
1 tablespoon lemon juice	(about 20)
1 teaspoon curry powder	

1. Use about 20 of the largest spinach leaves; save the remainder for another use, such as a spinach salad. Blanch the spinach leaves in a small saucepan of boiling water just until they soften slightly, about 15 seconds. Drain well in a colander. In a small bowl, combine the olive oil, lemon juice, and curry powder.

2. Prepare a medium fire in a covered charcoal or gas grill. Oil the grill rack. Dip the scallops into the oil mixture to coat, then wrap each one in a spinach leaf. Thread the spinach-wrapped scallops onto small metal skewers or soaked bamboo skewers, using the skewer to help secure the spinach wrapping. Dip the pineapple chunks in the remaining oil mixture and add to the ends of the skewers.

3. Grill the scallop and pineapple kebabs, turning occasionally, until the scallops are just opaque in the center and the pineapple is lightly tinged with brown, about 8 to 10 minutes. Serve directly from the skewers.

Grilled Lobster with Tarragon Vinaigrette

This is a fabulous way to eat lobster! If you are squeamish about splitting them yourself, ask the fishmonger to do so, but be sure to refrigerate and be ready to cook the lobsters within a couple of hours. Alternatively, you can first plunge them into boiling water for a couple of minutes, then split them. If you have fresh tarragon, use some sprigs as a garnish.

4 Servings

½ cup olive oil
3 tablespoons lemon juice
2 tablespoons minced shallots
1 tablespoon minced fresh tarragon or
   1 teaspoon dried
2 teaspoons Dijon mustard

¼ teaspoon salt
¼ teaspoon freshly ground pepper
4 live lobsters (about 1½ pounds
   each)
Lemon wedges

1. Prepare a medium-hot fire in a covered charcoal or gas grill. Oil the grill rack. In a small bowl, whisk together 7 tablespoons of the olive oil with the lemon juice, shallots, tarragon, mustard, salt, and pepper.
2. Split the lobsters in half lengthwise. Remove and discard the gray intestinal tract, the gills, and the sand sac in the head. Reserve any red roe or green tomalley that you find and stir it into the tarragon vinaigrette. Crack the lobster claws. Brush the lobsters with the remaining 1 tablespoon of the oil.
3. Grill the lobsters, cut sides down, for 4 minutes. Turn and grill 4 minutes longer. Turn again and grill until the lobster meat is translucent throughout but still juicy, about 3 to 4 minutes.
4. Drizzle the cut sides of the lobster with the tarragon vinaigrette and serve with lemon wedges.

Chapter Seven

Vegetables

Of all foods for grilling, vegetables are probably the most exciting and far and away my personal favorites. From peppers to eggplant, and potatoes to zucchini, almost any vegetable that will not fall through the grids is wonderful on the grill. In fact, grilling is such a terrific way to cook vegetables that I almost always add them any time I'm grilling meat, chicken, or fish, and often have grilled vegetables as the main course itself.

With just a sprinkling of salt and pepper and a light brushing of oil, grilled vegetables become meltingly tender and attractively browned. The natural sugars in vegetables caramelize to heighten the flavors. And the end result is some of the best low-fat food on earth.

In combination, grilled vegetables can easily become the main course, such as in our Grilled Tuscan Bread Salad, Grilled Greek Sandwiches, or Grilled Tofu and Vegetable Kebabs. For special occasions and parties, all manner of sauces and seasoned oils or butters can enhance grilled vegetables even further.

Because vegetables are often grilled without peeling, be sure to wash them thoroughly and pat dry first. Then apply a light brushing of oil to keep them from sticking to the grill. Soft vegetables can be completely cooked on the grill, but firm ones, such as potatoes and sweet potatoes, need precooking. Use a medium-hot or hot fire and cook briefly. When skewering vegetables, choose combinations that have almost the same cooking time or use separate skewers for each type of vegetable.

Grilled Belgian Endive

Belgian endives are delicate and costly little vegetables, but are worth every penny when grilled to a delicious golden brown tenderness.

4 Servings

---

3 tablespoons olive oil
1½ teaspoons chopped fresh thyme
  leaves or ½ teaspoon dried

4 Belgian endives (½ pound total)
Salt and freshly ground pepper

---

1. Prepare a medium-hot fire in a covered charcoal or gas grill. In a small dish, combine the olive oil and chopped thyme. Cut the Belgian endives in half lengthwise and brush all over with the seasoned oil.

2. Grill the endives, turning occasionally and brushing with any remaining oil, until fork-tender and tinged with brown, about 6 to 8 minutes. Season with salt and pepper to taste. Serve hot, warm, or at room temperature.

Grilled Asparagus with Orange Vinaigrette

As the harbinger of spring, asparagus could become your favorite "first-of-the-season" grilled vegetable, especially with a light orange vinaigrette and grilled orange slices as suggested here. When buying the vegetable, look for stalks of consistently medium thickness. There are two ways of trimming asparagus. You can use a vegetable peeler to peel the stalks to within about 3 inches of the tip, a method that uses the whole stalk, but takes some time to do. Or you can simply snap off the stalk at the point that it naturally breaks, which means you lose 2 or 3 inches of stalk.

3 to 4 Servings

---

1 pound fresh asparagus
1 small seedless orange, thinly sliced
2 tablespoons vegetable oil
2 tablespoons walnut, hazelnut, or vegetable oil

1 tablespoon orange juice
1 tablespoon red wine vinegar
¼ teaspoon salt
⅛ teaspoon freshly ground pepper

---

1. Prepare a medium-hot fire in a covered charcoal or gas grill. Oil the grill rack. Trim the asparagus either by peeling the stalks or snapping off the ends. Brush the asparagus and the orange slices with the 2 tablespoons vegetable oil. In a small bowl, whisk together the walnut oil, orange juice, vinegar, salt, and pepper.
2. Lay the asparagus spears perpendicular to the long grids (so they don't fall through) and grill, turning often with tongs, until softened and tinged with brown, about 9 to 11 minutes. Grill the orange slices, turning once or twice, until softened and tinged with brown, about 3 to 5 minutes.
3. Arrange the asparagus and orange slices on a platter and drizzle the vinaigrette over all. Serve warm or at room temperature.

Grilled Lemon Broccoli

When broccoli is grilled, the florets take on a wonderful smoky tenderness with crispy edges. It is one of those firmer vegetables, though, that must be boiled for a couple of minutes first.

4 to 6 Servings

---

1 large bunch of broccoli (about 1½ pounds)
¼ cup plus 2 tablespoons olive oil
1 large garlic clove, crushed in a press

1 tablespoon minced shallots
1 lemon, sliced
1 tablespoon lemon juice
Salt and freshly ground pepper

---

1. Cut the broccoli into spears with 2-inch stems. Cook the broccoli in a large saucepan of boiling salted water 2 minutes, or until barely crisp-tender. Drain into a colander and rinse under cold running water to stop further cooking. Shake the spears gently to rid the florets of excess water, then drain well on paper towels. (The broccoli can be prepared several hours ahead and set aside at room temperature.)
2. In a small bowl, combine the olive oil, garlic, and shallots. Let stand 30 minutes.
3. Prepare a medium-hot fire in a covered charcoal or gas grill. Brush the broccoli with some of the flavored oil. Grill, turning occasionally and brushing with more oil, until the stalks are tender and the florets are tinged with brown, about 6 to 8 minutes. Brush both sides of the lemon slices with the remaining flavored oil and grill, turning once, until tinged with brown, about 1 minute.
4. Arrange the broccoli on a platter or serving plates, sprinkle with the lemon juice, and garnish with the grilled lemon slices. Season with salt and pepper to taste. Serve warm or at room temperature.

Corn in a Cloak

There are several methods of grilling corn, but this one is easiest on the cook since the eaters husk their own ears. The husks act as a natural moisturizer to produce sweet, almost steamy corn with a light smoky flavor.

3 or 6 Servings

6 ears of fresh corn on the cob   Melted butter, optional
Salt and freshly ground pepper

1. Gently pull the husks back from the corn, but do not detach. Pull off and discard the corn silk, then return the corn husks to their original position covering the ear. Soak the corn in water to cover for 20 to 30 minutes.
2. Prepare a medium barbecue fire in a covered charcoal grill. Push the coals to one side. Or prepare an indirect fire in a gas grill according to the manufacturer's directions.
3. Grill the corn on the side away from the coals, turning frequently, until the corn kernels are tender, about 20 to 25 minutes.
4. Serve with salt, pepper, and melted butter, if desired.

Corn in the Nude

This method works best for freshly picked corn, which has lots of natural moisture. When grilled in this manner, the corn develops an intensely sweet and smoky flavor, heightened with a light brushing of cumin-flavored butter.

3 or 6 Servings

---

6 ears of fresh corn on the cob
3 tablespoons butter, melted
½ teaspoon ground cumin

¼ teaspoon salt
¼ teaspoon freshly ground pepper

---

1. Prepare a medium fire in a covered charcoal or gas grill.
2. Meanwhile, remove the husks and silk from the corn, but leave the stalks to use as handles. Stir together the butter, cumin, salt, and pepper. Brush about half of the seasoned butter over the corn kernels.
3. Grill, turning often and brushing with the remaining seasoned butter, until the corn kernels are tender and lightly browned, about 15 to 20 minutes.

Grilled Eggplant and Mozzarella Sandwiches

This is probably my favorite summer sandwich. It is dependent upon good oil, fresh herbs, and the best rolls you can find. If the eggplant is garden-fresh, you can skip the salting.

4 Servings

---

1 large or 2 smaller eggplant (about 1½ pounds total weight)
Salt
⅓ cup extra-virgin olive oil
2 large garlic cloves, minced
2 tablespoons chopped fresh basil, plus 8 whole sprigs
1 tablespoon chopped fresh oregano or 1 teaspoon dried

½ teaspoon freshly ground pepper
1 large ripe tomato, sliced about ¼ inch thick
4 Portuguese or other similar sandwich rolls, split
6 ounces mozzarella cheese, thinly sliced

---

1. Cut the eggplant into ½-inch slices. Sprinkle liberally with salt and set in a colander to drain for 20 minutes. In a small bowl, combine the olive oil, garlic, chopped basil, chopped oregano, and pepper. Let stand 15 minutes.

2. Prepare a medium-hot fire in a covered charcoal or gas grill. Rinse the eggplant under cold water and pat the slices dry with paper towels. Brush the eggplant and tomato slices on both sides with some of the flavored oil.

3. Grill the eggplant, turning occasionally and brushing with more oil, until tender and nicely browned, about 15 minutes. About 2 minutes before the eggplant is done, brush the cut sides of the rolls with any remaining flavored oil and set at the edge of the grill. Add the tomato slices and grill, brushing again with any remaining oil, just until the rolls are lightly toasted and the tomato is warmed and beginning to soften, 1 to 2 minutes.

4. Assemble the sandwiches by layering the grilled eggplant, cheese, and tomato slices on the bottoms of the rolls. Season with additional salt and pepper if desired and top each sandwich with a couple of sprigs of basil before covering with the top half of the roll.

Grilled Portobello Mushrooms

Portobellos are the giants of the mushroom family; some reaching 6 to 8 inches in diameter. Their meaty texture and woodsy flavor are deeply enhanced by grilling. In Italy, grilled portobellos are served as a main course, much as we might eat a steak. Serve smaller ones (about 3 inches) whole for a really spectacular first course or side dish, and slice larger grilled mushrooms to toss with pasta for an excellent meatless main course.

4 Servings

---

2 tablespoons butter
2 tablespoons olive oil
2 garlic cloves, crushed through a
  press
1 tablespoon chopped fresh tarragon or
  1 teaspoon dried

2 teaspoons lemon juice
1 pound portobello mushrooms
  (about 8)
1 tablespoon Cognac or brandy

---

1. In a small saucepan, melt the butter with the olive oil, garlic, and tarragon. Stir in the lemon juice. Remove from the heat and cover to keep warm.
2. Prepare a medium-hot fire in a covered charcoal or gas grill. Wipe the mushrooms clean with damp paper towels. Brush both sides with some of the flavored butter and oil. Grill, turning once and brushing with some of the remaining butter, until browned and fork-tender, about 12 to 15 minutes total.
3. Stir the Cognac into the remaining flavored butter and drizzle over the grilled mushrooms.

Grilled Jack Cheese-Stuffed Frying Peppers

This is a grilled variation on chiles rellenos, using frying peppers, but if you can find fresh poblano chiles, so much the better. It is a wonderful side dish that can be turned into a vegetarian main course when served with a tomato salsa or Grilled Tomato Sauce (p. 189).

6 Servings

---

6 poblano or Italian frying peppers
1 tablespoon vegetable oil

4 ounces Monterey Jack cheese with ja-lapeño peppers

---

1. Prepare a medium-hot fire in a covered charcoal or gas grill. Brush the peppers with half of the oil and grill, turning often, until the skins are blackened and the peppers are tender, about 10 to 12 minutes. Place the peppers in a paper bag and let cool for 10 minutes. Peel away the blackened skin from the peppers and cut a small slit in the stem end. Insert a small knife and scrape off as many of the seeds as possible. Shake out the seeds. (The peppers can be roasted several hours ahead and refrigerated. Return to room temperature before continuing.)

2. Cut the cheese into 6 rectangular sticks or pieces small enough to fit into the slit in the peppers. Insert the cheese in the peppers, taking care not to break the peppers. (If the peppers should split, simply wrap them around the cheese and secure with wet toothpicks.) Brush the peppers with the remaining oil.

3. Grill, turning once with a spatula, until the peppers are tinged with brown and the cheese is melted, about 3 to 5 minutes.

Grilled Potato Halves

You can precook these potato halves in a conventional oven, a microwave, or in a pot of boiling water, just as long as they aren't overdone before grilling. It is also an excellent way to use leftover cooked whole potatoes. The best type to use are long, slender russets, since they make the prettiest presentation and have a fine texture.

4 Servings

---

2 garlic cloves, crushed through a press
2 tablespoons olive oil
½ teaspoon dried marjoram
½ teaspoon salt

¼ teaspoon freshly ground pepper
4 long slender russet potatoes, scrubbed and halved lengthwise (6 to 8 ounces each)

---

1. In a small bowl, combine the garlic, olive oil, marjoram, salt, and pepper. Let stand at least 30 minutes or up to 2 hours.

2. Cook the potatoes until just tender, about 30 minutes in a preheated 350 degree oven, on High for about 10 minutes in a microwave oven, or about 15 minutes in a large pot of boiling salted water. The potatoes can be cooked several hours ahead. (If using leftover refrigerated cooked potatoes, bring them to room temperature before grilling.)

3. Prepare a medium-hot fire in a covered charcoal or gas grill. Brush the potatoes all over with some of the seasoned oil. Grill, turning occasionally and brushing with the remaining oil, until lightly browned, about 13 to 15 minutes.

Grilled Hash Browns

Preformed seasoned shredded "hash brown-style" potato "patties" are now widely available in the frozen food section. When grilled, they are really good.

6 Servings

---

1 (15- or 16-ounce) package seasoned
  shredded potato patties

---

1. Prepare a medium-hot fire in a covered charcoal or gas grill. Partially thaw the potato patties 10 minutes at room temperature.

2. Grill the patties, turning once with a wide spatula, until golden and crispy, with brown grill marks on both sides, about 15 minutes total.

Grilled Herbed Potato Salad

This potato salad is so delicious that it can easily become a main course, especially if you toss in some cubed ham or leftover roast beef.

4 Servings

1½ pounds small red potatoes
¼ cup olive oil
1 tablespoon chopped fresh rosemary
  or 1 teaspoon dried
3 tablespoons mayonnaise
2 tablespoons dry white wine
1 tablespoon white wine vinegar
2 teaspoons Dijon mustard

½ teaspoon salt
¼ teaspoon freshly ground pepper
⅓ cup thinly sliced scallions
3 tablespoons chopped parsley, preferably flat-leaf

3 to 4 branches fresh rosemary, optional

---

1. Cook the potatoes in a large saucepan of boiling salted water until just tender, 8 to 10 minutes. Drain well. (The potatoes can be precooked several hours ahead and set aside at room temperature.)

2. In a shallow dish, combine the olive oil and rosemary. Let stand at least 30 minutes or up to 2 hours. In another small bowl, whisk together the mayonnaise, wine, vinegar, mustard, salt, and pepper. Let stand at least 20 minutes or refrigerate up to 2 hours; return to room temperature before using.

3. Prepare a hot fire in a covered charcoal or gas grill. Roll the potatoes in the rosemary oil, then thread onto metal skewers. If using fresh rosemary branches, dampen them under cold water and toss onto the coals just before cooking.

4. Grill the potatoes, turning occasionally and brushing with any remaining flavored oil, until tender and tinged with brown, about 5 to 7 minutes.

5. Place the potatoes in a mixing bowl. Add the flavored mayonnaise, scallions, and parsley. Toss to combine. Season with additional salt and pepper to taste. Serve the salad warm or at room temperature.

Grilled Ratatouille

Grapevine cuttings add an even richer taste to the traditional vegetables that make up a classic ratatouille. Presented in an array on a platter, this is practically a whole meal, especially if you add some fresh mozzarella and a basket of Grilled Garlic Crostini (p. 25). A hinged grill basket, though not necessary, makes turning the vegetables a breeze.

6 Servings

¼ cup plus 2 tablespoons extra-virgin olive oil

2 garlic cloves, crushed through a press

2 tablespoons chopped fresh basil or 1½ teaspoons dried

1 tablespoon chopped fresh oregano or ¾ teaspoon dried

1 tablespoon chopped fresh summer savory or ¾ teaspoon dried

1 medium-sized eggplant (about 1 pound), sliced diagonally ½ inch thick

1 large zucchini (about ½ pound), sliced diagonally ½ inch thick

1 large crookneck squash (about ½ pound), sliced diagonally ½ inch thick

1 large red bell pepper, cut into 1-inch strips

1 large sweet onion, such as Vidalia, sliced ¼ inch thick

Salt and freshly ground pepper

1½ tablespoons balsamic vinegar

3 or 4 handfuls grapevine cuttings, optional

1. In a small dish, combine the olive oil, garlic, chopped basil, oregano, and savory.
2. If you have them, soak the grapevine cuttings in cold water for at least 30 minutes. Prepare a medium-hot fire in a covered charcoal or gas grill. Brush both sides of all of the vegetables with the flavored oil, then place in a hinged grill basket or directly on the grill. Grill the vegetables, turning occasionally and brushing with any remaining flavored oil, until tender and tinged with brown, about 10 to 12 minutes total.
3. Arrange the vegetables on a large platter. Season with salt and pepper to taste. Drizzle the balsamic vinegar over the grilled vegetables. Serve warm or at room temperature.

Blackened Scallions

Often used as a garnish or as one of several ingredients, scallions, also known as green onions, are so fabulous when grilled that they deserve to star as a vegetable on their own. A drizzle of peppery vinaigrette complements the blackened onion flavor. Try to find scallions of approximately the same size; those about ¼ to ½ inch in diameter are the easiest to grill. Serve these with plain grilled steaks or chops.

4 Servings

---

2 large bunches of scallions
3 tablespoons olive oil
1 tablespoon red wine vinegar
¼ teaspoon Tabasco or other hot
    sauce

¼ teaspoon salt
¼ teaspoon freshly ground pepper

---

1. Prepare a medium-hot fire in a covered charcoal or gas grill. Oil the grill rack. Trim the scallions to leave about 6 inches of green parts. Brush them with 1 tablespoon of the olive oil. In a small bowl, whisk together the remaining olive oil, vinegar, Tabasco, salt, and pepper.
2. Grill the scallions, turning with tongs, until softened and with some blackened edges all over, about 3 to 4 minutes total.
3. Arrange the grilled scallions on a platter. Drizzle the vinaigrette over them.

Grilled Molasses-Glazed Sweet Potato Slices

If you thought sweet potatoes were just for Thanksgiving, this will change your mind. Thinly sliced and brushed with a molasses glaze, these crisp-tender sweet potatoes are an excellent accompaniment to grilled chicken, turkey, or pork. If you have leftover whole baked sweet potatoes, they can be sliced about ¼ inch thick and grilled in the same way.

4 Servings

---

2 large sweet potatoes (about 1 pound total)

3 tablespoons vegetable oil

1 tablespoon molasses

¼ teaspoon salt

¼ teaspoon freshly ground pepper

---

1. Prepare a medium fire in a covered charcoal or gas grill. Oil the grill rack. Peel the sweet potatoes and cut them into thin lengthwise slices about ⅛ inch thick.

2. In a small bowl, stir together the oil, molasses, salt, and pepper until blended. Brush on both sides of the sweet potato slices.

3. Grill, turning occasionally with a wide spatula, until the sweet potatoes are golden brown and crisp on the outside and tender on the inside, about 10 to 14 minutes.

Grilled Acorn Squash with Cranberry Port Sauce

Precook the squash halves as directed here earlier in the day, then finish them off on the grill. If you want to make this a main course, fill the squash cavities with crumbled cooked sausage and bread stuffing instead of cranberry sauce. The cranberry sauce is good on its own as a condiment for Thanksgiving dinner, too.

4 Servings

1½ cups fresh cranberries

⅓ cup port wine

⅓ cup sugar

1 tablespoon minced candied ginger

2 teaspoons grated orange zest

2 acorn squash (about 1 pound each)

2 tablespoons vegetable oil

---

1. In a medium nonreactive saucepan, combine the cranberries, port, and sugar. Bring to a boil over medium-high heat, stirring to dissolve the sugar. Stir in the ginger and orange zest. Reduce the heat and simmer, stirring often, until the berries have popped and the sauce is thickened slightly, 6 to 8 minutes. Let the sauce cool completely. (The sauce can be made 3 days ahead and refrigerated. Return to room temperature before using.)

2. Cut the unpeeled squash in half lengthwise and scoop out all of the seeds and fibers. Shave a small slice off the bottom of each squash half so it will sit without wobbling. Place the squash, cut side up, in a shallow microwave-safe baking dish. Pour about ½ cup water into the dish, then cover tightly with plastic wrap. Microwave on High 10 minutes. Turn the dish 90 degrees and microwave 5 minutes,

---

or until the squash is just fork-tender. (Alternatively, bake the squash, covered with foil, in a preheated 400 degree oven 30 to 35 minutes. The squash can be cooked early in the day and set aside at room temperature.)

3. Prepare a medium-hot fire in a covered charcoal or gas grill. Oil the grill rack. Brush the squash with the vegetable oil and grill, cut side down, 10 minutes. Turn, fill each of the cavities with cranberry sauce, and grill until the squash is fork-tender, about 8 to 10 minutes longer. Serve with any remaining sauce on the side.

Grilled Green Tomatoes with Grilled Tomato Sauce

This is the recipe to use the night before the first frost is forecast, when your vines are still laden with both red and green tomatoes that have to be harvested right away. The red tomatoes are first grilled along with peppers and onions, then mixed to make a savory sauce. The green tomatoes are breaded in cornmeal and grilled to a golden brown crispness. Top them with red tomato sauce for a special treat.

4 Servings

---

2 medium-sized green tomatoes (about
  ¾ pound)
¼ cup flour
¼ cup yellow cornmeal
½ teaspoon salt
¼ teaspoon freshly ground pepper

¼ teaspoon cayenne
1 egg
1 tablespoon vegetable oil
½ recipe (2 cups) Grilled Tomato
  Sauce, optional (recipe follows)

---

1. Cut the tomatoes into ½-inch-thick slices. Pat dry. In a shallow dish, mix together 2 tablespoons of the flour with the cornmeal, salt, pepper, and cayenne. In another shallow dish, whisk the egg with the oil. Dust the tomato slices with the remaining 2 tablespoons flour, dip in the egg, and then dredge in the cornmeal mixture to coat completely. Set the slices on a rack to dry for about 30 minutes.
2. Prepare a medium-hot fire in a covered charcoal or gas grill. Oil the grill rack. Grill the tomatoes, turning once carefully with a wide spatula, until golden brown and crisp on the outside and softened on the inside, about 10 to 12 minutes total.
3. Serve the tomatoes with Grilled Tomato Sauce spooned on top, if desired.

Grilled Tomato Sauce

The addition of the grilled red pepper adds a depth to the sauce and also heightens the color. Spoon the sauce over Grilled Green Tomatoes (p. 188), Grilled Herbed Polenta (p. 26), or toss with about 12 ounces of cooked pasta. Season the sauce with basil or cilantro, depending upon whether you are in an Italian or a Mexican mood. Leftovers will keep in the refrigerator for several days.

Makes about 4 cups

---

2 red bell peppers, halved
1 sweet onion, such as Vidalia, cut
    into ½-inch slices
3 pounds ripe tomatoes
4 garlic cloves, peeled
⅓ cup plus 2 tablespoons olive oil
2 tablespoons balsamic vinegar

½ teaspoon salt
¼ teaspoon freshly ground pepper
¼ teaspoon Tabasco or other hot
    sauce
⅓ cup chopped fresh basil or ¼ cup
    chopped fresh cilantro

---

1. Prepare a medium-hot fire in a covered charcoal or gas grill. Brush the peppers, onion, tomatoes, and garlic cloves with 2 tablespoons of the olive oil. Wrap the garlic in a piece of heavy-duty aluminum foil to make a small packet. Set the packet on the edge of the grill and roast, turning occasionally, until the garlic is softened and tinged with brown, about 15 minutes.

2. Meanwhile, grill the peppers and onion in the center of the grill, turning often, until the pepper skins are blackened and the onions are golden, about 10 to 12 minutes total. Place the peppers in a paper bag and let cool 10 minutes. While

(continued on next page)

(continued from previous page)

the peppers are cooling, grill the tomatoes, turning often, until they are slightly softened and the skins are tinged with brown, about 3 to 5 minutes total.

3. Peel, seed, and coarsely chop the tomatoes and the peppers, placing them and any accumulated juices in a mixing bowl. Chop the onion and add to the bowl.

4. In a small bowl, mash the roasted garlic to a paste. Whisk in the remaining ⅓ cup olive oil, the vinegar, salt, pepper, and Tabasco. Add to the vegetables along with the chopped basil and stir to blend. Let the sauce stand at least 15 minutes or up to 1 hour at room temperature before using.

Grilled Greek Sandwiches

Summer squash and peppers are fabulous when grilled, and this Greek sandwich highlights the vegetable so very well. Serve with a cold rice salad.

4 Servings

⅓ cup olive oil
2 garlic cloves, crushed through a press
1 tablespoon chopped fresh mint
2 teaspoons chopped fresh thyme leaves or ½ teaspoon dried
¼ teaspoon salt
½ teaspoon freshly ground pepper

¾ pound zucchini (about 2 medium)
¾ pound yellow crookneck squash (about 2 medium)
1 red bell pepper
1 green bell pepper
2 large pita breads, partially split to make a pocket
4 ounces crumbled feta cheese

1. Prepare a medium-hot fire in a covered charcoal or gas grill. In a small dish, combine the olive oil, garlic, mint, thyme, salt, and pepper. Cut the zucchini and crookneck squash into long diagonal slices, each about ½ inch thick. Cut the red and green peppers into 1½-inch-wide strips. Brush the squash and pepper slices liberally with the flavored oil.

2. Grill the vegetables, turning often and brushing with more oil, until nicely browned and very tender, about 12 to 15 minutes. A couple of minutes before the vegetables are done, heat the pitas by placing them at the edge of the grill.

3. To assemble, brush the insides of the pitas with any remaining oil, then stuff with the vegetables and add the cheese.

Grilled Tuscan Bread Salad

Bread salad, called panzanella *in the Tuscany region of Italy, is a simple blend of fine ingredients: quality bread, fresh pepper and tomatoes, and the best vinegar and olive oil. Grilling makes them even better. This is traditionally served as a first course or as part of a mixed antipasto with, perhaps, a bowl of good olives on the side.*

6 Servings

1 small yellow bell pepper, halved
1 small red bell pepper, halved
1 small green bell pepper, halved
2 pounds ripe firm tomatoes (about 6 tomatoes)
¾ cup plus 2 tablespoons extra-virgin olive oil
1 loaf (10 to 12 ounces) Italian bread, cut into ¾-inch-thick slices
1 red onion, coarsely chopped
¼ cup plus 2 tablespoons balsamic vinegar

4 garlic cloves, minced
⅓ cup chopped fresh basil, plus a few sprigs for garnish
½ teaspoon salt
¼ teaspoon freshly ground pepper
4 ounces fresh mozzarella cheese, cut into ½-inch cubes, optional
1 head of romaine lettuce, torn into large pieces
1 head of radicchio, torn into large pieces

1. Prepare a hot fire in a covered charcoal or gas grill. Brush the yellow, red, and green peppers and the tomatoes with 2 tablespoons of the olive oil. Grill, turning occasionally, until the vegetables are softened and the skins are blackened, about 3 to 4 minutes for the tomatoes and about 6 to 8 minutes for the peppers. Place the peppers in a paper bag and let cool 10 minutes.

2. Meanwhile, grill the bread slices until lightly toasted on both sides, about 1 to 1½ minutes total. Cut or tear the bread into rough ¾-inch pieces.

3. Peel and discard the skins and seeds from the tomatoes and peppers. Coarsely chop the vegetables and place in a large mixing bowl, adding any tomato juices that accumulate on the cutting board. Add the bread and red onion to the bowl.

4. In a small bowl, whisk together the remaining ¾ cup olive oil, the vinegar, garlic, chopped basil, salt, and pepper. Add to the bread and vegetables and toss to mix thoroughly. Let stand 20 minutes at room temperature. Add the cheese, toss, and let stand 20 to 30 minutes longer.

5. On a large platter, make a bed of torn leaves of romaine and radicchio. Spoon the salad and juices over the lettuce. Grind additional fresh pepper over the salad and garnish with sprigs of fresh basil.

Grilled Tofu and Vegetable Kebabs

Extra-firm tofu, when drained of excess moisture, grills so nicely to a smoke-tinged flavor that you may never miss the meat in these kebabs. The vegetables can be varied as long as they cook in approximately the same time as the tofu. Trimmed broccoli florets, which cook more quickly than the stems, can be purchased in bags in the produce section or at the salad bar in the market. Serve the skewers atop a bed of rice.

4 Servings

---

1 container (12 to 16 ounces) extra-firm tofu, cut into 1-inch slices

¼ cup soy sauce

¼ cup dry sherry

2 tablespoons rice vinegar

2 tablespoons Asian sesame oil

2 garlic cloves, crushed through a press

2 tablespoons minced fresh ginger

½ pound broccoli florets (about 2 cups)

1 large red bell pepper, cut into 8 strips

---

1. Place the tofu in a single layer on a baking sheet lined with several thicknesses of paper towels. Cover the tofu with several more thicknesses of paper towels and another baking sheet to weight it down. Let the tofu stand until excess water is drained out, 1 or 2 hours. Cut the tofu into 1-inch cubes.

2. In a shallow dish large enough to hold the tofu, combine the soy sauce, sherry, vinegar, sesame oil, garlic, and ginger. Add the tofu and stir to coat completely. Refrigerate, covered, for at least 3 hours or up to 24 hours.

3. Prepare a medium-hot fire in a covered charcoal or gas grill. Oil the grill rack. Remove the tofu from the marinade; add the broccoli and red pepper to the marinade and toss to coat. Thread the tofu and vegetables onto metal skewers, alternating the ingredients. Grill, turning occasionally and brushing with any remaining marinade, until the tofu is lightly browned and the vegetables are lightly browned and tender, about 10 to 13 minutes.

Chapter Eight
Smoking

Home smoking is fast growing in popularity because it tastes terrific and is a relatively low-fat way to enjoy favorite meats, poultry, and seafood. Though it takes time, smoking is particularly easy, since all you really have to do is add fuel once in a while and spend the rest of the time working up an appetite. In my family, we have smoked everything from our Thanksgiving turkey to a Fourth of July brisket, and everyone always raves about the food.

Offset and water home smokers—albeit not the same as commercial smokers or old-time country pit-smokers—are easy to use and offer wonderful flavor combined with an entertaining way to spend a day. Be sure to follow the directions on your unit for preparing the fire and water pan, if there is one. Do not open the lid any more than absolutely necessary, since this will dramatically alter the temperature and allow the smoke to escape. Keep an eye on the temperature gauge and add fuel as needed. Smoked foods will be cooked through and can be tested with an instant-reading thermometer, but some other traditional tests will not apply, since smoked pork may be pink even though it is thoroughly cooked.

Offset smokers can also be used as conventional covered grills. They are especially well suited to recipes that require the use of an indirect or low fire.

Southern-Style Smoked Chicken

Not too spicy, this gentle herb mix gives a Southern flavor to a whole smoked chicken. Cut-up chicken and even boneless breasts can be coated and smoked in place of the whole bird done here, but the time will be a couple of hours less. I like this chicken served with a sweet potato salad dressed with a cider vinaigrette, or with chunky homemade applesauce.

6 Servings

---

2 teaspoons dried thyme leaves

2 teaspoons dried marjoram

1 teaspoon dried rosemary

1 teaspoon dried sage leaves

1 teaspoon dried basil

1 teaspoon salt

1 teaspoon freshly ground pepper

1 whole roasting chicken (4 to 5 pounds)

½ cup bourbon

4 to 6 handfuls hickory wood chips

---

1. In a small bowl, combine the thyme, marjoram, rosemary, sage, basil, salt, and pepper. Rinse the chicken inside and out and pat it dry. Rub the herb mixture all over the chicken, inside and out. Refrigerate the chicken at least 2 hours and up to 12 hours. Return to room temperature before smoking.

2. Prepare the smoker according to the manufacturer's directions. Soak the hickory chips in cold water for at least 30 minutes, then add to the smoker. Add the bourbon to the water in the water pan of the smoker. Smoke the chicken breast side up and without turning 4 to 5 hours, until the internal temperature registers 185 degrees on an instant-reading thermometer.

3. Let the chicken rest at least 10 minutes before carving. Serve warm or at room temperature.

Hotter 'n Hell Smoked Beef Brisket

This is a really incendiary rub for beef. It is recommended for those who really understand the word hot. The slight sweetness of the barbecue sauce is the ideal antidote for the fieriness of the rub. I like to serve this meat with creamy coleslaw and big soft rolls for making barbecue sandwiches. Adding some barbecue sauce to the water pan in the smoker lends additional flavor to the meat.

8 to 10 Servings

---

2 tablespoons sugar
1 teaspoon salt
1 teaspoon paprika
½ teaspoon cayenne
½ teaspoon freshly ground black
    pepper
½ teaspoon ground celery seeds
¼ teaspoon ground white pepper
¼ teaspoon grated nutmeg

¼ teaspoon ground cloves
1 whole beef brisket, well trimmed
    (5 to 6 pounds)
3 cups Sweet and Sour Barbecue Sauce
    (recipe follows)
¼ cup water

4 to 6 handfuls hickory or mesquite
    wood chips

---

1. In a small dish, mix together the sugar, salt, paprika, cayenne, black pepper, celery seeds, white pepper, nutmeg, and cloves. Rub this seasoning mixture all over the brisket. Refrigerate, covered, at least 4 hours and up to 24 hours. Return to room temperature before smoking.

2. Prepare the smoker according to the manufacturer's directions. Soak the wood chips in cold water for at least 30 minutes. Just before smoking, place about half of the chips in the smoker. Add 1 cup of the Sweet and Sour Barbecue Sauce to the water in the water pan of the smoker.

---

3. Smoke the meat without turning 5 to 6 hours, until the brisket is fork-tender and beginning to fall apart, adding the remaining wood chips to the smoker about halfway through the cooking time.

4. Remove the meat from the smoker, wrap in aluminum foil, and let rest at least 15 minutes before slicing thinly across the grain. Place the meat slices in a baking pan, coat with the remaining barbecue sauce mixed with ¼ cup water, and cover the pan with aluminum foil. (The recipe can be prepared to this point several hours ahead.)

5. Preheat the oven to 350 degrees. Bake the covered pan of brisket in the sauce until heated through, 30 to 45 minutes.

Sweet and Sour Barbecue Sauce

This is a good sauce for barbecued pork chops or ribs. Since it keeps well in the refrigerator for weeks, I often make it in quantity. Packed in decorative jelly jars, the sauce makes a very nice little hostess gift.

Makes about 3 cups

---

3 tablespoons vegetable oil
1 medium onion, finely chopped
1 large celery rib, finely chopped
2 garlic cloves, minced
1 teaspoon grated fresh ginger
1 teaspoon paprika
2 cups bottled chili sauce

⅓ cup honey
¼ cup cider vinegar
1 cup apple cider or apple juice
2 tablespoons Worcestershire sauce
2 tablespoons dark rum
½ to 1 teaspoon Tabasco sauce, or
    more to taste

---

1. Heat the oil in a medium nonreactive saucepan. Add the onion, celery, and garlic and cook over medium heat until softened, about 3 minutes. Stir in the ginger and paprika and cook 30 seconds. Add the chili sauce, honey, vinegar, cider, Worcestershire, and rum.

2. Bring to a boil, reduce the heat to medium-low, and simmer uncovered, stirring occasionally, until slightly thickened, about 30 minutes. Season to taste with Tabasco. Use immediately or refrigerate up to 4 weeks.

Smoked Turkey Mole

Though mole is usually served as a sauce for roasted poultry, here the same flavors are used in a tasty rub for a smoked turkey. The same smoking method can be used without the mole rub, of course, for a plain smoked turkey. Either way, leftovers make superb sandwiches.

10 to 12 Servings

---

3 tablespoons chili powder

2 tablespoons brown sugar

2 teaspoons onion powder

2 teaspoons unsweetened cocoa powder

1½ teaspoons salt

¾ teaspoon ground cumin

¾ teaspoon garlic powder

¾ teaspoon dried oregano

½ teaspoon cayenne

1 (15-pound) whole turkey

4 to 6 handfuls mesquite chips

---

1. In a small dish, mix together the chili powder, brown sugar, onion powder, cocoa, salt, cumin, garlic powder, oregano, and cayenne.

2. Rinse the turkey and pat dry. Rub the mixed mole spices all over the turkey, inside and out. Let the turkey stand 30 minutes at room temperature or refrigerate up to 12 hours, returning to room temperature before cooking.

3. Prepare the smoker according to the manufacturer's directions. Soak the wood chips in cold water for at least 30 minutes. Just before cooking, place about half of the wood chips in the smoker.

4. Smoke the turkey breast side up without turning 7 to 8 hours, until the internal temperature registers 185 degrees on an instant-reading thermometer. Add more wood chips to the smoker as needed. Let the turkey rest at least 10 minutes before carving into thin slices. Serve warm or at room temperature.

Jerk Smoked Pork Chops

You can also smoke boneless chops, but I think that the bone adds flavor to the meat. The rub below is also excellent on chicken, or goat if you want to be really authentic to the Jamaican roots of this now popular kind of barbecue.

6 Servings

---

2 tablespoons brown sugar
1 tablespoon onion powder
2 teaspoons ground allspice
1 teaspoon garlic powder
1 teaspoon salt
1 teaspoon cayenne
1 teaspoon ground sage

1 teaspoon ground thyme
½ teaspoon ground cinnamon
¼ teaspoon grated nutmeg
3 pounds center-cut pork chops, cut
   ¾ inch thick

4 to 6 handfuls mesquite chips

---

1. In a small dish, mix together the brown sugar, onion powder, allspice, garlic powder, salt, cayenne, sage, thyme, cinnamon, and nutmeg to make the jerk seasoning.

2. Rub the jerk seasoning on both sides of the pork chops. Let stand at room temperature 1 hour or refrigerate up to 4 hours. Return to room temperature before cooking.

3. Prepare the smoker according to the manufacturer's directions. Soak the wood chips in cold water for at least 30 minutes, then add to the smoker.

4. Smoke the pork chops without turning until cooked through, about 3 hours. (The pork may be pink near the edge due to the smoking, but it should be white to the bone.)

Smoked Apple-Sage Game Hens

The apple-sage glaze gives a luxurious sheen and sophisticated flavor accent to the game hens or their French relatives, poussins. I really love to serve these at room temperature at an early autumn tailgate picnic, accompanied by a wild rice and grape salad. Applewood or other fruitwood chips complement the glaze.

6 Servings

---

6 Cornish game hens or poussins
  (about 1 pound each)
Salt and freshly ground pepper
¼ cup apple jelly
¼ cup dry white wine

1 teaspoon dried sage leaves

4 to 6 handfuls apple- or other fruitwood chips

---

1. Prepare the smoker according to the manufacturer's directions. Soak the wood chips in cold water for at least 30 minutes. Just before cooking, place the chips in the smoker.

2. Rinse the hens and pat them dry. Season them lightly inside and out with salt and pepper. Smoke the hens breast side up 2 hours.

3. While the hens are smoking, make the glaze by heating the jelly, wine, and dried sage in a small nonreactive saucepan over medium heat just until the jelly melts, about 2 minutes. After 2 hours of smoking, brush the hens with the glaze and smoke 30 minutes. Brush again and smoke 30 to 45 minutes longer, or until the internal temperature registers 185 degrees on an instant-reading thermometer. Serve the hens warm or at room temperature.

Carolina Pork Barbecue

One of the main differences between Carolina and Texas barbecue is the lack of tomato in the Carolina sauce. For serving, the meat is torn, or pulled, into shreds and heaped into rolls for perhaps the best sandwiches ever. The pork marinates for a day, so leave lots of time; but a nice side note for entertaining is that the meat is even better cooked a day ahead and reheated.

6 to 8 Servings

---

1 tablespoon vegetable oil
2 tablespoons chili powder
1 teaspoon ground cumin
1 teaspoon paprika
½ teaspoon dry mustard
½ cup water
½ teaspoon salt
½ teaspoon freshly ground pepper
¼ teaspoon cayenne

½ cup cider vinegar
2 tablespoons Worcestershire sauce
2 tablespoons honey
2 bottles or cans of beer (12 ounces each)
1 pork butt (5 to 6 pounds)

4 to 6 handfuls hickory wood chips

---

1. Heat the oil in a medium saucepan over medium-low heat. Add the chili powder, cumin, paprika, and dry mustard. Cook, stirring, 1 minute. Stir in the water, salt, pepper, cayenne, vinegar, Worcestershire, honey, and 1 bottle of beer. Bring just to a boil, reduce the heat to medium-low, and simmer 5 minutes. Let the marinade cool. (The marinade can be prepared up to 3 days ahead and refrigerated.)
2. Place the pork butt in a large mixing bowl. Pour half of the marinade over the meat, reserving the remainder for a sauce. Cover and refrigerate 24 hours, turning occasionally. Return to room temperature before smoking.

3. Prepare the smoker according to the manufacturer's directions. Soak the hickory chips in cold water to cover for at least 30 minutes, then add about half of the wet chips to the smoker. Add the remaining bottle of beer to the water in the smoker water pan. Smoke the meat for 6 hours, adding the remaining wet wood chips after 3 hours. Remove the meat from the smoker.

4. The meat can now be finished either in the smoker or in the oven. Tightly wrap the meat in a large piece of heavy-duty aluminum foil and smoke an additional 2 hours or place in a roasting pan and bake 2 hours in a preheated 325 degree oven until the meat is falling-apart tender.

5. Let the meat rest about 30 minutes in the foil. Then tear it into shreds with 2 forks or with your hands. Serve immediately with the remaining sauce on the side. Or refrigerate overnight, then reheat covered and coated with more sauce in a preheated 325 degree oven until hot, about 30 minutes.

Five-Spice Ribs

This simple rub gives a complex flavor to smoked ribs, but is also good on chicken or pork chops. Chinese five-spice powder is readily available in the spice sections of large supermarkets and in Asian groceries.

6 to 8 Servings

---

2 tablespoons Chinese five-spice powder

2 teaspoons garlic powder

2 teaspoons onion powder

1 teaspoon cayenne

6 pounds pork spareribs

4 to 6 handfuls mesquite wood chips

---

1. In a small bowl, combine the five-spice powder, garlic powder, onion powder, and cayenne. Rub the spices over both sides of the ribs. Refrigerate at least 2 hours and up to 6 hours. Return to room temperature before smoking.

2. Prepare the smoker according to the manufacturer's directions. Soak the wood chips in cold water at least 30 minutes. Just before cooking, put about half of the chips in the smoker.

3. Smoke the ribs, turning once, 3½ to 4½ hours, or until cooked through. (Cut through in the center to check for doneness: The pork may look slightly pink at the edge due to the smoking, but it should be cooked to the bone.) Add the remaining wood chips to the smoker about halfway through the cooking time. To serve, cut the racks into 2- or 3-rib sections.

Home-Smoked Salmon

This is not like commercial smoked salmon, but rather a moist, smoky version of grilled salmon. It is perfect for a main course, especially when topped with a dab of dill butter. For a drier, more potent smoked salmon to use as an appetizer on crackers, the fish can be left in longer. The preliminary brining is important to firm up the fish and add texture. Whitefish and even bluefish can be smoked in a similar way.

4 to 6 Servings

½ cup coarse sea salt or kosher salt

½ cup sugar

1½ quarts water

1½ pounds unskinned salmon fillets

4 to 6 handfuls hickory or mesquite wood chips

---

1. In a large nonaluminum dish or bowl, stir the salt and sugar into the water until dissolved. Add the fish and submerge in the brine. Cover and refrigerate 12 to 24 hours.

2. Prepare the smoker according to the manufacturer's directions. Soak the wood chips in cold water for at least 30 minutes, then add them to the smoker. Remove the fish from the brine, rinse under cold running water, and pat dry.

3. Smoke the fish, skin side down, about 1½ hours, until cooked through but not dry. (If a drier, more potently flavored salmon is preferred, leave in the smoker 1 hour longer.) Serve warm as a first course or chilled as an appetizer.

Smoked Shellfish Salad

The shellfish can also be served on their own as appetizers or even as a main course, but the lightness of the salad greens and the mild vinaigrette make a pleasing contrast to the smokiness. The proportions of seafood can be varied to suit your tastes. Use mesquite chips, because the strong flavor of hickory or even fruitwood chips will overpower the shellfish.

4 to 6 Servings

---

12 oysters in the shell

12 small hard-shell clams, such as
   littlenecks

12 large or jumbo shrimp in the shell

12 large sea scallops

1 head of red leaf lettuce

2 tablespoons white wine vinegar

1 tablespoon minced shallot

1½ teaspoons chopped fresh tarragon
   or ½ teaspoon dried

1 teaspoon Dijon mustard

¼ cup plus 2 tablespoons extra-virgin
   olive oil

Salt and freshly ground black pepper

2 to 3 handfuls mesquite wood chips

---

1. Prepare the smoker according to the manufacturer's directions. Soak the wood chips in cold water for at least 30 minutes. Open the oysters and clams, leaving them on the half shell. (Your fishmonger can do this for you, but you will need to be ready to smoke the clams shortly thereafter.) Thread the shrimp and scallops onto metal skewers.

2. Just before cooking, add the wood chips to the smoker. Smoke the shellfish until all are cooked through, about 1 hour.

3. Meanwhile, tear the lettuce into bite-sized pieces and place it in a salad bowl. Whisk together the vinegar, shallot, tarragon, and mustard. Whisk in the olive oil. Season the vinaigrette with salt and pepper to taste.

4. At serving time, toss the lettuce with the vinaigrette. Divide among 4 or 6 serving plates. Arrange the smoked clams and oysters in their shells atop the greens. Remove the shrimp and scallops from the skewers; shell the shrimp. Arrange the shrimp and scallops on the greens. Serve warm or at room temperature.

Index

A

Acorn squash, grilled, with cranberry port sauce, 186
All-American barbecued chicken, 39
All-American barbecue sauce, 42
Appetizers and snacks, 15–37
  BBQ wings, 19
  broccoli and potatoes with beer cheese fondue, grilled, 36
  cheese and bean tostadas, grilled, 32
  chicken kebabs, yogurt- and mint-grilled, 16
  chicken satay, grilled Indonesian, 17
  cocktail franks, sweet and sour, 23
  French toast with maple-mustard sauce, grilled, 35
  garlic crostini, grilled, 25
  pizza, pepperoni and cheese, quick grilled, 29
  pizza, white clam, wood-fired, 30
  polenta, grilled herbed, 26
  quesadillas, grilled, 31
  rumaki, grilled, 24
  scallop and grapefruit kebabs, grilled, 21
  sesame chicken tidbits with sweet and sour dipping sauce, grilled, 18
  shrimp cocktail, grilled, 22
  spiedini, grilled, 28
  stuffed grape leaves, grilled, 27
  tomato and basil bruschetta, grilled, 33
  tuna kebabs with wasabi and pickled ginger, grilled, 20

Apple(s)
  peppered, grilled venison steaks with, 96
  -sage game hens, 203
  and sage-stuffed pork roast, grilled, 100
Aromatic flavorings, 4–6
Asparagus with orange vinaigrette, grilled, 170
Avocado guacamole, simple, 73

B

Bananas, Polynesian pork kebabs with pineapple and, 106
Barbecue(d). *See also* Pork, spareribs
  chicken
    all-American, 39
    drumsticks, Texas finger-lickin', 46
    wings, 19
  ham steaks, ginger-peachy, 107
  lamb, Hunan, 121
  meat loaves, mother's, 86
  pork, Carolina, 204
  pork steaks, East St. Louis, 104
  sauce
    all-American, 42
    chuck wagon, 79
    doctored-up, 105
    Memphis rib, 117
    sweet and sour, 199
Basque chicken, skewered, 48
BBQ wings, 19
Bean and cheese tostadas, grilled, 32
Beef

brisket
> grill-smoked, with chuck wagon barbe-
> > cue sauce, 78
> hotter 'n hell smoked, 198

burger(s)
> bruschetta, 90
> Cajun, 88
> and the works, the best, 87

chuck roast, grill-smoked country, 80

ribs
> Big Ben's, 84
> Korean, 85

roast, herbed boneless, with horseradish
> sauce, 82

salad, Thai grilled, 74

steak
> au poivre with caramelized leeks,
> > grilled, 69
> fajitas, 72
> flank, teriyaki, with grilled shiitake
> > mushrooms, 70
> sticks, zesty orange, 71
> tenderloin, with a trio of sauces, grilled, 76

Beer cheese fondue, grilled broccoli and pota-
> toes with, 36

Belgian endive, grilled, 169

Best burger and the works, the, 87

Big Ben's ribs, 84

Blackened red snapper fillets, 147

Blackened scallions, 184

Brats and circus onions, grilled, 112

Bread
> crostini, garlic, grilled, 25
> salad, grilled Tuscan, 192

Brisket of beef
> grill-smoked, with chuck wagon barbecue
> > sauce, 78

hotter 'n hell smoked, 198

Broccoli
> lemon, grilled, 171
> and potatoes with beer cheese fondue,
> > grilled, 36

Bruschetta
> burgers, 90
> tomato and basil, grilled, 33

Burger(s)
> beef
> > bruschetta, 90
> > Cajun, 88
> > and the works, the best, 87
> > Italian sausage, grilled, 110
> > lamb, grilled, in pita pockets, 133
> > turkey, Thanksgiving in July, 62
> > veal, Swedish, 95

C

Caesar's chicken salad, grilled, 54

Cajun burgers, 88

Calf's liver and onions, grilled, 91

Caper crème fraîche, grilled salmon steaks
> with, 144

Carolina pork barbecue, 204

Catfish with cornmeal and pecan crust,
> grilled, 138

Cauliflower, Tandoori-style chicken with pep-
> pers and, 47

Charcoal fire
> controlling the heat of, 8
> preparing, 6
> starter methods for, 6–7

Cheese
> and bean tostadas, grilled, 32
> fondue, beer, grilled broccoli and potatoes
> > with, 36

Cheese (*cont.*)
and pepperoni pizza, quick grilled, 29
quesadillas, grilled, 31
Chicken
"Cordon Bleu," grilled, 45
barbecued, all-American, 39
Basque, skewered, 48
with cauliflower and peppers, Tandoori-
style, 47
drumsticks, barbecued, Texas finger-
lickin', 46
Jamaican jerk, 43
liver rumaki, grilled, 24
patties Provençal, grilled, 50
salad
Caesar's, grilled, 54
Vietnamese chicken noodle, grilled,
52
satay, grilled Indonesian, 17
Southern-style smoked, 197
stuffed with lemons and sage, grilled, 40
tidbits, sesame, with sweet and sour dipping sauce, grilled, 18
West Coast grilled, 44
wings, BBQ, 19
yogurt- and mint-grilled kebabs, 16
Chowder, grilled monkfish, 142
Chuck roast, grill-smoked country, 80
Chuck wagon barbecue sauce, 79
grill-smoked brisket with, 78
Cilantro, grilled rainbow trout stuffed with
citrus and, 151
Clam pizza, white, wood-fired, 30
Coconut
lamb steaks, curried, 127
mahimahi with macadamia butter and
toasted, grilled, 139

Corn
in a cloak, 172
in the nude, 173
Couscous salad with mint vinaigrette, 135
Moroccan lamb and, grilled, 134
Covered grills
advantages of, 1–2
attachments for, 11
safety tips, 9–10
sources for, 12–13
types of, 2–3
Crabapple- and sage-glazed quail, grilled, 65
Crab(s)
cakes with spicy mayonnaise, grilled, 158
soft-shell, grilled, with mustard butter, 160
Cranberry
ketchup, 63
port sauce, grilled acorn squash with, 186
Crème fraîche
caper, grilled salmon cakes with, 144
to make your own, 145
Crostini, garlic, grilled, 25
Cucumber-yogurt sauce, 129
souvlaki with, 128
Curried coconut lamb steaks, 127

D
Deviled pork cutlets, grilled, 114
Dill-mustard salmon roast, grilled, 146
Doctored-up barbecue sauce, 105

E
East St. Louis barbecued pork steaks, 104
Eggplant
Japanese, and grilled tuna on soba noo-
dles, 154
and mozzarella sandwiches, grilled, 174

F

Fajitas, steak, 72
Fennel and lemon grilled pork tenderloin, 99
Feta cheese, grape leaves stuffed with, 27
Fish, 136–57. *See also specific types of fish*
Five-spice ribs, 206
Flank steak with grilled shiitake mushrooms, teriyaki, 70
Fondue, beer cheese, grilled broccoli and potatoes with, 36
Franks. *See also* Hot dog, the ultimate cocktail, sweet and sour, 23
French toast with maple-mustard sauce, grilled, 35
Fuels, 4
    sources for, 13–14

G

Game hens
    with mango salsa, grilled, 64
    smoked apple-sage, 203
Garlic
    crostini, grilled, 25
    and oregano boneless leg of lamb, 122
Ginger-peachy barbecued ham steaks, 107
Grapefruit and scallop kebabs, grilled, 21
Grape leaves, grilled stuffed, 27
Greek sandwiches, grilled, 191
Green tomatoes, grilled, with grilled tomato sauce, 188
Grilling, tips for, 10–11
Guacamole, simple, 73

H

Ham
    grill-smoked, 108
    steaks, ginger-peachy barbecued, 107

Hash browns, grilled, 179
Herb(ed)
    boneless roast beef with horseradish sauce, 82
    potato salad, grilled, 180
    -stuffed grilled turkey breast, summer, 58
Horseradish sauce, herbed boneless roast beef with, 82
Hot dog. *See also* Franks
    the ultimate, 111
Hotter 'n hell smoked beef brisket, 198
Hunan barbecued lamb, 121

I

Indonesian chicken satay, grilled, 17
Italian sausage
    burgers, grilled, 110
    and pepper hero, grilled, 113

J

Jack cheese-stuffed frying peppers, grilled, 177
Jamaican jerk chicken, 43
Jambalaya, grilled shrimp and sausage, 162
Jerk chicken, Jamaican, 43
Jerk smoked pork chops, 202

K

Kebabs. *See also specific vegetables*
    chicken, yogurt- and mint-grilled, 16
    lamb and summer vegetable, 130
    melon and lamb, 132
    pork
        red onion, brandied fig, and, 103
        with pineapple and bananas, Polynesian, 106
    scallop and grapefruit, grilled, 21

Kebabs (*cont.*)
  sea scallop and pineapple, green, 166
  tofu and vegetable, grilled, 194
  tuna, with wasabi and pickled ginger,
    grilled, 20
Ketchup, cranberry, 63
Korean beef ribs, 85

L
Lake Logan ribs, 118
Lamb
  burgers in pita pockets, grilled, 133
  chops with spicy mint pesto, grilled,
    124
  Hunan barbecued, 121
  leg of, boneless
    and couscous salad, grilled, 134
    garlic and oregano, 122
    kebabs, melon and, 132
    souvlaki with cucumber-yogurt sauce,
      128
    spiedini, rosemary and, 131
    and summer vegetable kebabs, 130
  rack of, spiced, 123
  steaks
    curried coconut, 127
    with Thai hot and sweet sauce, 126
Leeks, caramelized, grilled steak au poivre
  with, 69
Lemon(s)
  broccoli, grilled, 171
  chicken stuffed with sage and, grilled
    whole, 40
  and fennel grilled pork tenderloin, 99
Liver and onions, grilled, 91
Lobster with tarragon vinaigrette, grilled,
  167

M
Macadamia butter, grilled mahimahi with
  toasted coconut and, 139
Mackerel with Romesco sauce, grilled, 140
Mahimahi with toasted coconut and macada-
  mia butter, grilled, 139
Mahogany turkey legs, 60
Mango salsa, grilled game hens with, 64
Maple-mustard sauce, grilled French toast
  with, 35
Mayonnaise, spicy, grilled crab cakes with,
  158
Meat loaves, mother's barbecued, 86
Melon
  and lamb kebabs, 132
  and prosciutto, grilled, 34
Memphis dry ribs, 116
Memphis rib sauce, 116
Mint
  pesto, spicy, 125
    grilled lamb chops with, 124
  and yogurt-grilled chicken kebabs, 16
Molasses
  -glazed sweet potato slices, grilled, 185
  -rum country-style ribs, 119
Mole, smoked turkey, 201
Monkfish chowder, grilled, 142
Moroccan lamb and couscous salad, grilled,
  134
Mother's barbecued meat loaves, 86
Mozzarella and eggplant sandwiches, grilled,
  174
Mushrooms
  portobello, grilled, 176
  shiitake, grilled, teriyaki flank steak with, 70
Mustard
  butter, grilled soft-shell crabs with, 160

-dill salmon roast, grilled, 146
-tarragon veal cutlets, grilled, 94

N
Noodles
   chicken salad, grilled Vietnamese, 52
   soba, grilled tuna and Japanese eggplant
      on, 154

O
Onion(s)
   circus, grilled brats and, 112
   liver and, grilled, 91
   red, pork loin, and brandied fig kebabs,
      103
Orange
   beef sticks, zesty, 71
   vinaigrette, grilled asparagus with, 170
Oregano and garlic boneless leg of lamb, 122

P
Pasta
   pesto, grilled seafood brochettes on, 150
   salad, turkey sausage, grilled, 55
   shrimp and sea scallops on, grilled, 165
Peachy barbecued ham steaks, ginger-, 107
Peppered apples, grilled venison steaks with,
   96
Peppered peach glaze, grill-smoked turkey
   with, 56
Pepperoni and cheese pizza, quick grilled, 29
Peppers, frying, grilled jack cheese-stuffed,
   177
Pepper(s), sweet bell
   and Italian sausage hero, grilled, 113
   red, Tandoori-style chicken with cauli-
      flower and, 47

Pesto
   pasta, grilled seafood brochettes on, 150
   spicy mint, 125
   grilled lamb chops with, 124
Pineapple
   Polynesian pork kebabs with bananas
      and, 106
   and sea scallop kebabs, green, 166
Pizza
   pepperoni and cheese, quick grilled, 29
   white clam, wood-fired, 30
Polenta, herbed, grilled, 26
Polynesian pork kebabs with pineapple and
   bananas, 106
Pork. *See also* Ham; Sausage
   barbecue, Carolina, 204
   burgers
      grilled Italian sausage, 110
      Southwest, 109
   chops
      grill-smoked, 102
      jerk smoked, 202
   cutlets, grilled deviled, 114
   kebabs
      red onion, brandied fig, and, 103
      with pineapple and bananas, Polyne-
         sian, 106
   ribs, molasses-rum country-style, 119
   roast, apple- and sage-stuffed, grilled, 100
   spareribs
      five-spice ribs, 206
      Lake Logan, 118
      Memphis dry, 116
      real good, 115
   steaks, barbecued, East St. Louis, 104
   tenderloin, lemon and fennel grilled, 99
Portobello mushrooms, grilled, 176

Potato(es)
  and broccoli with beer cheese fondue,
    grilled, 36
  halves, grilled, 178
  hash browns, grilled, 179
  salad, grilled herbed, 180
Prosciutto and melon, grilled, 34

Q

Quail, crabapple- and sage-glazed, grilled, 65
Quesadillas, grilled, 31

R

Ratatouille, grilled, 182
Red snapper, blackened fillets of, 147
Ribs. *See also* Beef, ribs; Pork, spareribs
  pork, molasses-rum country-style, 119
Rice, skewered Basque chicken with, 48
Romesco sauce, 140
Rumaki, grilled, 24

S

Sage
  -apple game hens, smoked, 203
  and apple-stuffed pork roast, grilled, 100
  and crabapple-glazed quail, grilled, 65
  grilled whole chicken stuffed with lemons
    and, 40
Salad
  beef, Thai grilled, 74
  chicken
    Caesar's, grilled, 54
    noodle, grilled Vietnamese, 52
  couscous, with mint vinaigrette, 135
    Moroccan lamb and, grilled, 134
  Niçoise, grilled tuna, 156
  potato, grilled herbed, 180

shellfish, smoked, 208
taco, grilled turkey, 61
turkey sausage pasta, grilled, 55
Tuscan bread, grilled, 192
Salmon
  cakes with caper crème fraîche, grilled,
    144
  home-smoked, 207
  roast, grilled mustard-dill, 146
Salsa, mango, grilled game hens with, 64
Sandwiches. *See also* Burgers
  eggplant and mozzarella, grilled, 174
  Greek, grilled, 191
  Italian sausage and pepper hero, grilled,
    113
  spiedini, grilled, 28
Sauce
  barbecue
    all-American, 42
    chuck wagon, 79
    doctored-up, 105
    Memphis rib, 117
    sweet and sour, 199
  cranberry port, grilled acorn squash with,
    186
  cucumber-yogurt, 129
    souvlaki with, 128
  horseradish, herbed boneless roast beef
    with, 82
  maple-mustard, grilled French toast with,
    35
  Romesco, 140
  Thai hot and sweet, lamb steaks with, 126
  tomato, grilled, 189
    grilled green tomatoes with, 188
Sausage
  brats and circus onions, grilled, 112

Italian
  burgers, grilled, 110
  and pepper hero, grilled, 113
  and shrimp jambalaya, grilled, 162
  turkey, pasta salad, grilled, 55
Scallions, blackened, 184
Scallop(s)
  and grapefruit kebabs, grilled, 21
  sea
    grilled shrimp and, on pasta, 165
    and pineapple kebabs, green, 166
Seafood. *See also* Fish; Shellfish
  brochettes on pesto pasta, grilled, 150
Sesame chicken tidbits with sweet and sour
    dipping sauce, grilled, 18
Shellfish, 158–67. *See also specific types of
    shellfish*
  salad, smoked, 208
Shrimp
  cocktail, grilled, 22
  Español, grilled, 161
  with low country dipping sauce, grilled, 164
  and sausage jambalaya, grilled, 162
  and sea scallops on pasta, grilled, 165
Smokers, 3, 196
Soba noodles, grilled tuna and Japanese egg-
    plant on, 154
Southern-style smoked chicken, 197
Southwest pork burgers, 109
Souvlaki with cucumber-yogurt sauce, 128
Spareribs. *See* Pork, spareribs
Spiced rack of lamb, 123
Spiedini
  lamb and rosemary, 131
  grilled, 28
Spinach, in green sea scallop and pineapple
    kebabs, 166

Squash, acorn, grilled, with cranberry port
    sauce, 186
Steak(s). *See specific meats*
Summer herb-stuffed grilled turkey breast, 58
Swedish vealburgers, 95
Sweet and sour
  barbecue sauce, 199
  cocktail franks, 23
  dipping sauce, grilled sesame chicken tid-
    bits with, 18
Sweet potato slices, grilled molasses-glazed,
    185
Swordfish Siciliana, grilled, 148

T

Taco salad, grilled turkey, 61
Tandoori-style chicken with cauliflower and
    peppers, 47
Tarragon
  -mustard veal cutlets, grilled, 94
  vinaigrette, grilled lobster with, 167
Teriyaki flank steak with grilled shiitake
    mushrooms, 70
Texas finger-lickin' barbecued drumsticks, 46
Thai grilled beef salad, 74
Thanksgiving in July turkey burgers, 62
Tofu and vegetable kebabs, grilled, 194
Tomato(es)
  and basil bruschetta, grilled, 33
  compote, triple, grilled veal chops with, 92
  sauce, grilled, 189
    grilled green tomatoes with, 188
Tostadas, cheese and bean, grilled, 32
Trout
  grill-smoked, 152
  rainbow, stuffed with citrus and cilantro,
    grilled, 151

Tuna
  and Japanese eggplant on soba noodles,
    grilled, 154
  kebabs with wasabi and pickled ginger,
    grilled, 20
  salad Niçoise, grilled, 156
Turkey
  breast, summer herb-stuffed grilled, 58
  burgers, Thanksgiving in July, 62
  grill-smoked, with peppered peach glaze,
    56
  legs, mahogany, 60
  mole, smoked, 201
  sausage pasta salad, grilled, 55
  taco salad, grilled, 61
Tuscan bread salad, grilled, 192

U
Ultimate hot dog, the, 111

V
Veal
  burgers, Swedish, 95

chops with triple tomato compote,
  grilled, 92
cutlets, tarragon-mustard, grilled, 94
Vegetable(s), 168–95. *See also specific*
  vegetables
  Greek sandwiches, grilled, 191
  ratatouille, grilled, 182
  summer, and lamb kebabs, 130
  and tofu kebabs, grilled, 194
Venison steaks with peppered apples, grilled,
  96
Vietnamese chicken noodle salad, grilled, 52
Vinaigrette
  orange, grilled asparagus with, 170
  tarragon, grilled lobster with, 167

W
West Coast grilled chicken breasts, 44

Y
Yogurt
  -cucumber sauce, 129
    souvlaki with, 128
  and mint-grilled chicken kebabs, 16